Praise for Nell Stevens's

BLEAKER HOUSE

"A book that's simultaneously smart, lively and even, at points, unhinged. . . . Stevens charts a path of personal and professional exploration tinged with both sadness and humor."   —*Jezebel*

"An honest portrait of writerly neurosis."
—*San Francisco Chronicle*

"One of the most original, entertaining, and thought-provoking books I have ever read about the difficulty of writing a book."
—Rebecca Mead, NewYorker.com

"*Bleaker House* is so riveting and so much fun to read, I would have loved it even if it hadn't also been innovative and brilliant. Nell Stevens is an excellent writer, as well as great company, and I can't wait to read every book she writes."
—Kate Christensen, author of *The Great Man*, winner of the PEN/Faulkner Award for Fiction, and *Blue Plate Special*

"Fresh and spirited. . . . [A] delightful literary debut."
—*Kirkus Reviews*

"An entertaining, perverse and singular book."   —*The Observer*

"[Stevens] encounters not only an eccentric cast of outsiders but also the furious demands of her own creative self, in this true-life chronicle of loneliness and renewal."   —Oprah.com

"Quirky and engaging. . . . A captivating portrait of the creative life." —*BookPage*

"A romp of a book, a genre-defying feat of the imagination, and a pure pleasure to read." —Alison Pick, author of *Far to Go* and *Between Gods*

"A picaresque, recognisably human tale of a young woman's failure to follow through on the glaringly unrealistic goals she set herself." —*London Evening Standard*

"Stevens writes with considerable charm and winning honesty." —*The Guardian*

"The perfect read for anyone who has ever considered themselves 'a writer.'" —*The Sunday Times Style* (London)

"Hilarious and original, charming and engaging. I loved it." —Rebecca Wait, author of *The Followers* and *The View on the Way Down*

"An enthralling reflection on writing. . . . [A] confiding, edgy and ever-so-slightly horrifying book which I enjoyed so much I wolfed it in one sitting." —Caroline Sanderson, *Daily Express* (London)

"It's comforting to know that even without any of the distractions of normal life, even at the ends of the Earth, you can still end up whistling in the wind." —*Daily Mail* (London)

"[A] whimsical, good-humored, yearning-filled, thought-provoking read." —*Bustle*

Nell Stevens

BLEAKER HOUSE

Nell Stevens has a degree in English and creative writing from the University of Warwick, an MFA in fiction from Boston University, and a Ph.D. in Victorian literature from King's College London.

www.nellstevens.com

BLEAKER HOUSE

BLEAKER

CHASING MY NOVEL

ANCHOR BOOKS

A Division of Penguin Random House LLC

New York

HOUSE

TO THE END OF THE WORLD

Nell Stevens

FIRST ANCHOR BOOKS EDITION, FEBRUARY 2018

Copyright © 2017 by Nell Stevens

All rights reserved. Published in the United States by Anchor Books,
a division of Penguin Random House LLC, New York. Originally published in
hardcover in the United States by Doubleday, a division of Penguin Random
House LLC, New York, in 2017.

Anchor Books and colophon are registered trademarks of
Penguin Random House LLC.

Bleaker House is a work of both memoir and fiction. The memoir sections are based
on the author's recollections; however, she has changed the names and certain
features of some of the individuals about whom she has written, and has amended
chronologies and details of some of the events described. The fiction sections of
Bleaker House are just that: fiction. They are works of the author's imagination.

The Library of Congress has cataloged the Doubleday edition as follows:
Names: Stevens, Nell, author.
Title: Bleaker house : chasing my novel to the end of the world / Nell Stevens.
Description: New York : Doubleday, 2017.
Identifiers: LCCN 2016041607 (print) | LCCN 2016056564 (ebook)
Subjects: LCSH: Stevens, Nell, 1985– | Authors, English—21st century—Biography. |
Fiction—Authorship. | Falkland Islands—Description and travel. | BISAC:
BIOGRAPHY & AUTOBIOGRAPHY / Personal Memoirs. | TRAVEL / South America /
General. | BIOGRAPHY & AUTOBIOGRAPHY / Women.
Classification: LCC PR6119.T478 Z46 2017 (print) | LCC PR6119.T478 (ebook) |
DC 823/.92 [B]—DC23
LC record available at https://lccn.loc.gov/2016041607

Anchor Books Trade Paperback ISBN: 978-1-101-97286-1
eBook ISBN: 978-0-385-54156-5

Book design by Pei Loi Koay

www.anchorbooks.com

Printed in the United States of America
10 9 8 7 6 5 4 3 2 1

To Margaret and Richard

BLEAKER HOUSE

Prologue

A generous donor has made it possible for us to send most of our students abroad after they complete their degree requirements. Global Fellows in Fiction may go to any country and do there what they wish, for a typical stay of up to three months. The Global Fellowship adventure is not only intended to help Boston University's MFA candidates grow as writers, but also to widen eyes, minds, and hearts—from which better writing might eventually flow.

— BOSTON UNIVERSITY CREATIVE WRITING DEPARTMENT

This is a landscape an art-therapy patient might paint to represent depression: grey sky and a sweep of featureless peat rising out of the sea. The water is the same colour as the clouds; it is flecked by white-capped waves, spikes of black rock, and, intermittently, the silvery spines of dolphins. I pace from room to room in the empty house, testing out the silence with occasional noises: "Hi! Ha! Who! How!" My fingers are stiff with cold. When I open my notebook, I fumble with the pages; I struggle to grip the pen. I write the title of a journal entry: "Bleaker Island, Day One." Beneath it, an attempt at a beginning: "I am living alone on an island."

I spell it out to myself. I try to make sense of where I, astonishingly, am. What I've written sounds like a metaphor, so I clarify: "This is not a metaphor." I am living alone on an island, a real island in the Antarctic waters of the South Atlantic, and the name of the island is Bleaker.

I have been cold since the moment I woke up, stiff and groggy, fleetingly confused and turning over in my mind all the places I might be: at home, in London; in my student apartment in Boston; at my parents' house; my best friend's place; the hotel on Exmoor where I stayed—How long ago? Days? Weeks?—to be a bridesmaid at a wedding. The final option that occurred to me, least plausible, true, is that I was where I in fact was. I dressed in the chill—sweatpants over jeans over tights, woolly hiking socks pulled halfway up my calves—and scurried to the window. Behind the curtain, there it was: the island and, all around it, the sea.

I flew here yesterday, from Stanley, capital of the Falkland Islands, in a tiny plane. We juddered over the sea and over a blot of lumpy islands, then past a white beach crowded with penguins, before landing, softly, on grass. I stepped down from the plane to face a little hut and a sign that read, in crooked letters: "Welcome to Bleaker Island."

Now, I am the sole resident of a large, dark house. When I first arrived, I stood in the doorway to watch the sun drop out of the sky into the grey water, listening to the thick silence of this empty corner of the world.

I set about trying to make the place feel less empty, or at least, to revise the emptiness into something that feels as though it belongs to me. I unpack the few items of warm clothing I am not already wearing and take my food supplies to the kitchen, lining them up beside the microwave, each day's rations weighed out and counted in advance. Doors to unoccupied bedrooms I decide to keep closed. In the living room, there is a table large enough to host a dinner party for ten, and deep, bouncy sofas strewn with sheepskins: it is a room made for entertaining and company. It should be full of people, and it makes me panicky to be in there by myself, like a host awaiting guests who will never arrive.

The biggest space in the house was described in the online brochure I read before my arrival as a "sunroom," a conservatory tacked on to the front of the building. Hail is pelting the glass roof with a metallic-sounding din. Through rivulets of melting ice running down the windowpanes, the sunroom offers a panoramic view of the island to the north: waves chewing the edge of the settlement, farm buildings on the other side of a small bay, looming clouds interrupted by wheeling birds of prey. This is where I will write.

I convert a coffee table into a writing station, loaded with the tools I imagined in advance I'd need to build a novel: laptop, notebooks, tatty copy of *Bleak House*, pencil, pens. I position everything neatly, then worry that the orderliness will seem oppressive. I disarrange the objects, as though I had tossed them down without much thought. Still, somehow, the table feels like a set, the sunroom like a stage, and the island beyond like a gaping, vacant auditorium.

Later, I set out to begin my exploration of Bleaker. The house is on a narrow section, in the relative shelter of a hill, which I climb, bent into the wind and small shards of freezing rain. From the top, you can see the whole curve of the island: cliffs on the west side and a beach on the east, speckled with black-and-white dots that, when you walk towards them, bloom into penguins. They waddle and slither into the waves and run out again like delighted toddlers. Caracaras cluster overhead, eyeing anything that shines. I walk for hours and see only monosyllables: cliffs, birds, waves, sand, sheep, rock, moss.

A dream: You can see, on an island near yours, a plane. You watch yourself, on that other island, boarding the aircraft. But you know the person you are watching is not really you, because you are here, alone, on an island with no plane. You yell. You try to get the attention of the other you, or the pilot, and explain the mistake, but the wind swallows your voice and throws specks of saliva back into your mouth. The plane takes off and vanishes amongst clouds and circling albatrosses. The other you will get home, be welcomed back by family and friends, marry your future husband and write your novel, and nobody will ever know that you, the real you, are in fact still here, alone. Beside you on the beach, an elephant seal emits a long and fart-like groan.

In the applications I send out to Creative Writing MFA programmes in the States, two years before I find myself on the island, I quote Ted Hughes: "For me, successful writing has usually been a case of having found good conditions for real, effortless concentration." I want to do an MFA because I desperately want to concentrate, because it will mean I won't have to work in my draining, unrewarding office job, and because it will take me away from my friends and family in the UK to a place where I will know nobody from whom to demand distraction—but of course it doesn't. I am accepted into the one-year, intensive Fiction MFA at Boston University, where, as in London, life gets in the way. I make new friends, develop crushes, go on dates, and spend more time than I could possibly have imagined on the phone to Bank of America and Verizon and the BU International Students & Scholars Office. I worry about rent money and my tax return and my hair and my visa and whether the thing I said to my room-mate about the way her voice carries came out wrong.

At the end of the year, however, there is a chance of redemption. The programme ends in what it calls a "global fellowship": students are sent out into the world, wherever they choose to go, to spend three months living, exploring, writing. In March, there is an information session, which outlines the application process and exactly how much money we can expect to cover our trips; I become preoccupied with thoughts and plans and schemes for my fellowship. I don't want to waste it. I want to do it right. The absorbing vision of "effortless concentration" appears before me again, and I find myself pining for empty, remote places: snow plains, broad lakes, oceans, wherever there is more nothing than there is something and where, I imagine, I will finally do the thing I have spent my adult life hankering after, attempting, and interrupting: write a novel.

I wonder how productive, how focused, how effective I can be. On the phone to my mother I tell her, "I want to know how good at life I can be in a place where there are no distractions." After a long Boston winter, it is finally spring, and I am walking down Commonwealth Avenue in bright sunlight. Around me the city is busy and shiny and diverting.

"And where is that, exactly?" she asks.

"The Falklands," I say. "I think it's the Falklands."

Even as I make this statement—*I want to know how good at life I can be in a place where there are no distractions*—I question it. I wonder how naive I am being. Surely by now I should know that wherever I am, wherever I go, however determined, I can find ways to distract myself, to procrastinate, to put off the real labour of creating something with words.

It turns out, though, that I am not being naive. As I stand in the sunshine talking on the phone to my mother, watching cars and buses and students with cups of frozen yogurt go past, I cannot begin to conceive of how few distractions there will be on Bleaker Island.

"I'm going to the Falklands," I tell my friend Laura, who is a poet. "I'm going to live alone on an island and write a novel."

It is now April of the MFA year, and we are still in the process of putting together our fellowship applications. Laura and I are sitting in a seminar room, high up in one of the towers of Boston University, after a class on Arabic translations of Dickens. The windows frame the silver curve of the Charles sliding between brownstones and glassy office blocks. It is dusk and everything looks pink.

I open my laptop to show her a picture of the island, the tiny settlement perched on a narrow patch of land: the farmhouse, the shearing shed, the house by the water I'll be renting, and surrounding it, a bleak landscape of rocks and mud. I zoom in on satellite images of the cliffs, the beach and caves and empty space: it gives me a kind of vertigo to see it.

When I look at Laura for a reaction, I can't quite gauge her expression. She is applying to go to Brittany to translate the poems of Paol Keineg. Her fellowship, I am certain, will be picturesque. When I imagine it, she is eating croissants, drinking good coffee, and riding a blue bicycle around a clifftop village. She has planned a trip that has the potential to be both career-boosting, and actively pleasant.

"Bleaker Island?" she says. "You can call your novel *Bleaker House.*"

When I crow with excitement and tell her, delighted, that yes, I will, that's wonderful, she frowns and adds, "Nell, that was a joke."

Leslie Epstein, Director of Creative Writing at Boston University, is holding my fellowship application and looking at me over the top of it. His eyes are deep-set and reticent, and make me feel as though I have to earn the right to meet his gaze. When I do so, now, there is an amused glint there: not distinct enough to make me certain he is laughing at me, but enough to make me suspect it.

He reads my proposal back to me, in his creaky, mirthful voice: "There has never been a literary novel set in the Falkland Islands. What literature there is consists of poetry, non-fiction accounts of the war of 1982 between Britain and Argentina, and thrillers that use the conflict as a backdrop. When I discovered the lack of fiction set in these remote islands, it confirmed to me that if I could go anywhere in the world to live, and write, and observe, for an extended period of time, it would be the Falklands."

I can feel myself blushing at the sound of my own optimistic pitch. What seemed powerful and utterly convincing when I wrote it is now trite, naive, and arrogant. This is one of Leslie's great skills as a teacher: sometimes all he needs to do is walk into the room for you to understand where you've gone wrong.

He reads on. "It was their isolation that first drew me to the idea: this tiny colony of sheep farmers, most of whom self-identify as British, which has existed eight thousand miles from the UK for the past two hundred years. It is difficult and expensive to reach them, on an eighteen-hour military flight from a British air base. And at the end of that arduous journey, you arrive to find islands home to more soldiers than civilians, and where sheep outnumber humans by two hundred and fifty to one. Large areas of land are still littered with unexploded mines from the war. The temperature between May and October, winter in the Southern Hemisphere, is rarely above freezing, gales drive in weekly from the Atlantic, power is lost for days at a time. When I try to imagine how it would feel to stay there, I'm not sure whether claustrophobia or agoraphobia springs more pressingly to mind. I imagine the closeness of a community so distant from its purported motherland; the oppressiveness of being stuck on a small, militarized island with limited means of escape. Then I picture the emptiness of it: the unpopulated landscape and deserted minefields; the Antarctic ozone hole that causes extreme sunburn even on cloudy days."

Leslie lays the paper flat on the desk and smoothens the edges. "You can go anywhere in the world," he says. "People like to go to Europe. You could go to Southeast Asia."

I am discombobulated. Up until this meeting, I had been completely convinced by my case for the Falklands, and had jealously guarded the idea, worried someone else might steal it. Now, it seems perfectly obvious that I should be going to Rome, or Marrakech, or Cuba. I have a sudden vision of myself on the sunlit balcony of a crumbling old mansion in Havana, drinking mojitos, gazing down at the street and making occasional scribbles in the kind of notebook that everyone says Hemingway used, but which he actually didn't: she seems relaxed, this other me, and smug.

"But in the Falklands –" I start. "On Bleaker—"

Leslie interrupts. "You want to be alone," he says, and looks strangely sad.

"The thing I'm most scared of is getting depressed," I say.

I am with friends in London, the night before I begin my journey to the South Atlantic. We are drinking wine in a Hackney flat. I have finished my year in Boston and flown back to the UK to attend a wedding and dump three suitcases of clothes and books on the floor of my childhood bedroom at my parents' house.

It's hot. People are fanning themselves with coasters. My hair is sticking to the sweat on my temples. We take turns squeezing out onto the tiny balcony; over the rooftops of dimly lit estates, the city shines. It strikes me that even this—the heat, the sweat, the electric horizon—will soon be precious.

Everyone seems to have a strong opinion about what I am about to do.

The lawyer, who is stressed and overworked, thinks the isolation will be wonderful, a complete escape. "You can do yoga. You can meditate."

The ecologist wants to know about the wildlife, wants me to set up a blog.

The actor says, "It will be a chance to really get to know yourself," then, doubtfully, "but perhaps you know yourself quite well already?"

The primary-school teacher is the only one who downs her glass, looks me in the eye, and says, "Of course you'll get depressed. It's going to be fucking horrible. It will be cold and you won't have enough to eat. You got depressed house-sitting alone in Wales for a week."

Any Idiot Can Write a Book

n my first year as an undergraduate at the University of Warwick, the English Department secretary circulates an "opportunity." A production company is looking for contestants to participate in a new TV show. They are seeking unpublished writers who have completed a novel. The show will be modelled on *The Apprentice*. Each week, a writer will be voted off and sent home. At the end of the series, the winner will be given a "financial prize" (amount not stated) and their novel will be published (publisher unspecified). Applicants should respond with a CV, photo, and description of their writing. The name of the show is *Any Idiot Can Write a Book*.

I have just finished my gap-year novel: a tortured romance about a young woman in Northern India who falls in love with a Tibetan refugee. An agent has seen it and gently suggested that the story might be better if more things actually happened. I am not ready to accept this advice. Instead, I write a synopsis of a book in which nothing happens, set against a backdrop of glistening Himalayas, and send it off to the people behind *Any Idiot Can Write a Book.*

Two weeks later, I am taken in a taxi to a farmhouse on the outskirts of Stratford-upon-Avon, where I am filmed over several takes getting out of the car and walking up the garden path. The front door is open, because the cameraman is standing there, but I have to pretend to ring the bell and wait.

If I have had any suspicions that the premise behind *Any Idiot Can Write a Book* was flawed before I arrived, these are confirmed once we start the work of filming the show—which in fact is not a show at all, but a pilot that may or may not be developed and which we will shoot over the course of a single day. Aside from me, there is only one other contestant: a skinny Mancunian called Jake, who has a shakily drawn snake tattoo winding around his neck in the shape of a noose. The judge is an eminent literary critic of whom I've not heard. This is her farmhouse.

Jake and I are ushered into a barn that has been converted into a large study. We are told to sit at computers and type.

"Type what?" asks Jake.

"It doesn't matter what," the director says. "We're not focusing on the screens."

"Well then, what are you focusing on?" Jake responds.

The director says nothing.

Jake faces his keyboard and begins to jab at it with his forefingers. I turn to mine and pretend as best as I can to be hard at work on the novel I have already finished, but beyond frowning at my screen as I type nonsense into Word, it's unclear how exactly I should dramatize the moment. The essential issue with the premise of the show is apparent at once: there is nothing remotely interesting about observing people writing.

"Can you walk around the garden a bit?" the director asks me. "Can you look troubled?"

Trying to look both whimsical and perturbed, I meander between elaborate flower beds of hollyhocks.

"What's wrong?" a girl with a microphone asks.

"I'm . . . I'm worried about my novel," I try.

"What's worrying you?"

"Nothing happens in it."

The director interjects. "Let's try this one more time."

"What's wrong?" says the girl.

"I'm worried about my novel."

"What's worrying you?"

"Nothing happens."

We do this over and over.

"What's worrying you?"

"Nothing happens."

"What's worrying you?"

"Nothing happens."

By the final take, my distress is genuine.

In the afternoon, I read the opening scene of my novel in a recording booth—my voice will play over the footage of my dramatic typing—and sit on a bench under an umbrella in the drizzle answering questions about how much I want to be a writer (very much) and what it would mean to me to get through to the next round of *Any Idiot Can Write a Book* (as the day wears on, less and less). Just as it begins to get dark, we film the judging and elimination scene. Jake and I sit at the kitchen table opposite the critic, with our novels in front of us. I understand by now the ridiculousness of the situation, but still, I'm nervous. My hands and forehead are sweaty; my throat feels dry.

I read a scene from my book in which the two lovers meet

for the first time, in a temple in Dharamsala, surrounded by flickering candles and stray dogs. I try to keep my voice steady and expressive, but as I go on, it becomes increasingly raspy. I look up at the director to see if she wants me to start again from the top, but she is whispering something to the microphone girl and doesn't appear to have noticed.

Next, Jake reads a chapter of his novel, which is called *Bad Splatter* and follows the adventures of a happy-go-lucky drug dealer called Rad the Fucker.

The director interrupts. "You can't say that."

"What?"

"Fucker."

"But that's his name."

"Give him a new one."

Jake looks troubled, but eventually begins again and gets through his scene, in which Rad the Bastard drowns an adversary in liquid concrete on a building site.

"Thank you both," the critic says. "I know you've worked hard on these chapters. I'll start with Nell."

She absolutely loves my chapter. It is poignant, and romantic, and sad. The characters are robust and sensitively drawn, and the whole section is full of potential, suggestive of all the many things that might, at some point, start to happen. My face is getting hot; I try to nod seriously. Somehow, despite the praise, I feel unwell. I hold onto my manuscript so tightly the paper turns furry with sweat.

"Now, Jake." The critic turns to him and her face sets into a grimace. "I have to say, I was really disappointed by your work. I found it incredibly predictable. I've heard it a hundred times before."

"What?" Jake is half out of his chair. "That's not true."

"Drug dealers . . . concrete . . . I mean, it's all cliché, isn't it? It's one cliché after another."

"You haven't understood the project," he says. "Let me read it again." He picks up his pages and starts from the top.

"No need, Jake." She cuts him off. "There is absolutely no future for you on this show, or as a writer in any shape or form. You are untalented, unimaginative, offensive and tired."

I am sitting so tensely in my chair that my shoulders start to cramp. My gaze swivels between the two of them as they argue. Their voices are rising. Jake looks a little unhinged; his eyes begin to bulge. A shout of "You're a fraud!" is accompanied by a plume of spit that lands between us on the table. I might throw up.

"You can argue and shout," the critic snarls, "but it won't make your writing any more palatable."

Jake is on his feet now. "This is pathetic," he says. "This is a waste of my time." He turns, knocking his chair over behind him, and stamps out of the kitchen.

In the aftermath, the room is silent, and then the microphone girl says, "I think that was really good."

When everything is wrapped up, the microphone girl walks me to my taxi.

"Great day," she says. "You were just right. We think this could be a segment on *Richard and Judy,* actually. They've expressed interest."

"Is Jake OK?" I ask. I haven't seen him since he was eliminated at the kitchen table.

"Jake? Oh, he's fine."

"He seemed pretty upset."

"Yes, he was good, wasn't he?"

"Good?"

"Yes, we thought he did really well. Oh—you know that was staged, right? They were practising that scene all morning." When I look blank, she repeats herself. "It was staged. They rehearsed the whole argument. Jake was totally fine with it. He loved it."

My head is feeling thick and fuzzy. This information sinks in slowly. "It was staged," I repeat. And then, "But does that mean she didn't really like my book?"

"I thought someone had told you afterwards," the girl says. "Sorry. We had to keep you in the dark before and during, obviously, to get your reactions."

"Uh-huh."

"Which were great, by the way. You looked really happy, and then really shocked."

I nod. "I was," I say. "I was really shocked."

I sink into the taxi seat, ready to head back to Warwick and what turns out to be a severe bout of tonsillitis. I will be bedridden for a week and lose a tenth of my body weight, and by the end of it, I will have arrived, somehow, at the conclusion that it is important for things to happen in a novel.

Boston University Global Fellowship Proposal

Excerpts: Text and Subtext

1. There has never been a literary novel set in the Falkland Islands . . . When I discovered the lack of fiction set in these remote islands, it confirmed to me that if I could go anywhere in the world to live, and write, and observe, for an extended period of time, it would be the Falklands.

1. *I want to write—to be a writer—and still, at twenty-seven, don't know what exactly I want to say.*

2. When I contacted travel agents to get quotes and information for this trip, the general response was incredulity. Many don't actually

2. *I do not want to have a nice time. What I want—what I need—is to have the kind of time that I can convert into a book.*

operate in the colder season, when I plan to be there. Most tourists, they told me, arrive on cruise ships, offload for a day and leave before dark. The few independent visitors come in the warmer months, between November and April. I might have a nicer time, they suggested, gently, if I delayed my trip until the summer. They stopped short of asking me directly, "Why?"

3. It is hard to explain the appeal of loneliness to a writer; of isolation and disorientation, displacement and homesickness.

3. *I am scared that the life I want to lead, the life of a writer, is inevitably built on loneliness, and I need to know if I can hack it. If I can teach myself the art of loneliness, then perhaps the art of writing will come more easily to me. If I can break my habit of being distracted, maybe I'll also break my habit of writing novels that don't work.*

4. I want to go to a place, not just *where* I can write, but which I can *write about*. So much about the Falklands makes them a rich subject

4. *My peers from high school and university seem to have spent their twenties nimbly climbing the ladders of their respective careers: from med student to*

for stories: their extreme isolation, both geographically and culturally; the way the language has developed independently of British or American English to become something completely its own; the contrast between the Islanders and the soldiers on the vast British military base; the hardships and extremity of life lived in a place so remote. The fact that the islands are, according to the local government, "free from crime" makes them a ripe setting for drama of any sort. In a place where nothing criminal ever occurs, how would people respond to peculiar or sinister events? Two years ago, the bodies of two Chinese fishermen washed up on the shore of one of the more remote settlements; the strangeness of that occurrence, and the possibilities for ensuing mystery, suggest to me that the Falklands are brimming with potential for fiction.

trainee to junior doctor; law degree to bar school to pupillage to tenancy. Teachers. Scientists. Journalists. Successful young people who know where they are going. Meanwhile I have been pursuing this intangible goal of "becoming a writer" and I have nothing much to show for it. I do not, therefore, have the time or money to waste a second of my Global Fellowship. When it is over I will need to find a new job to support myself, and that will inevitably reduce my writing hours, and the goal that is always just out of reach will slip further and further away, and soon enough I will turn thirty and still not know what to say when people at parties ask me what I do, and at some point— when?—I will have to join the ranks of people who wanted to be writers but are now something else. In short, this trip needs to offer everything all at once: material and time, drama and silence, because otherwise I do not know what I will do. I need to leave the Falklands with a novel.

5. Jorge Luis Borges described the 1982 Falklands War as "two bald men fighting over a comb." I would like to spend my Global Fellowship exploring all the reasons why he might have been incorrect.

5. *I really hope he was incorrect.*

Closed to All Vehicles and Pedestrians

My journey to the Falkland Islands unfolds in increasing degrees of strangeness.

From London I fly to Santiago. It takes thirteen hours, overnight, and I share the economy cabin with the Chilean football team. They spend their time affably autographing shirts for other passengers. When I walk out of the airport in Chile the air is cold. It is late June, and I realize with a spasm of shivers that I've flown into a new hemisphere, a new season: it is suddenly winter.

From my hotel room: a view of the city and snow-capped Andes. The peaks of the mountains turning pink at dusk. Strains of Amy Winehouse drift up from the courtyard that make my skin prickle, familiar and strange. Fighting jet lag, trying to stay awake, I read Darwin's *Voyage of the Beagle*: August 27th, 1833, "I stayed a week in Santiago, and enjoyed myself very much."

The next day, after a restless night, I wake up late to the sounds of sirens and shouting. There's an angry crowd marching through the city. The ebullient receptionist at the hotel, Daniela, cautions me against going out—the park is closed in any case, she says—but she can't explain in English what the rally is about. I watch from the window of my room as armoured vehicles pass, streaked with brightly coloured paint. Later, it's quiet. I wander out into the city and find myself in a cloud of tear gas lingering from the recently dispersed protest: burning in my throat, stinging my eyes. Almost immediately, while my breath is still tight and my vision blurred, I experience a blossoming dread. Tomorrow I leave Santiago for the Falklands. I am going somewhere stranger, wilder, colder, and bleaker than I want to imagine. When Darwin arrived there, in the March of 1833, he found an "undulating land, with a desolate and wretched aspect." They were "miserable islands," he wrote, inhabited by "runaway rebels and murderers." I cough, and wipe my mouth, and squeeze water out of my eyes.

It would be easier, I think, to stay here for the duration of the fellowship, become friends with Daniela, learn Spanish, and do my writing at the terrace café outside Pablo Neruda's house with a view of the park and the city below. But then, what would I write? "Life is nice, the coffee is good, and everyone is kind." I could join the protests if they go on for another day, I think, get properly tear-gassed and write about that.

But the flight is booked for seven a.m., and I will be on it.

Later, I sit in the hotel courtyard in the last of the day's sun, watching cats hotfoot across tilting rooftops. Daniela brings out pisco sours and sweet, crumbling cookies. Sugar tingles in the back of my throat. It's hazy and I can barely make out the mountains.

. . .

On the plane from Santiago to RAF Mount Pleasant, East Falkland, I am the only woman. The rest of the seats are occupied by a Chilean fishing crew of stocky, rough-skinned men who occasionally stare at me with a dull curiosity. A strange landscape slides beneath the aircraft: beige grassland and blue lakes and white peaks. It is not so much like a different country as a different planet.

I dig through my hand luggage searching for the itinerary I put together before I left, and unfold it in my lap: white sheets that I convince myself still smell a little of the ink from the printer in the Boston University Library. It all looks so clean and easy written down: my route across the world is only a few inches long, from one side of the page to the other. There is a map of the Falklands archipelago, with the twin masses of its two largest islands, East and West Falkland, spread side by side like the wings of a butterfly pressed onto the paper. Around them, the smaller islands cluster, with names that seem lifted from adventure stories: Carcass, Lively, Pebble, Motley, Beaver, Barren, Bleaker, Ghost. I have put stars next to the places I will visit, and drawn little arrows between them, marking the direction of travel. I remember how unsure I was, when planning everything, where I should go and when and for how long, but it doesn't look that way written down: it all looks deliberate and certain, as though I knew exactly the right thing to do.

"I think I'll just go to straight to Bleaker," I told my mother. "I want to get straight to the isolation bit, to spend as much time as possible on my own. That's the interesting part."

"Yes," she said, "I know," and then paused so I could feel the weight of her scepticism. "But wouldn't it be better to meet some people first? To get a sense of the whole country? Don't you want to see how it all fits together?" When I gave no response, she said again, a little more forcefully, "I think it would be good for you to meet some *people*."

A compromise, then: I will spend the first few days at a settlement called Darwin, on the west side of East Falkland. It will be remote, very quiet, an indication of what is to come on Bleaker, like an isolation taster-course. From there, to satisfy my mother, I will go to Stanley, capital of the Falklands, and stay for a month in a guest house. I can research my novel in the government archives and at the museum; I can settle myself into the culture and lifestyle; and I can "meet some people." Then, finally, I will make it to Bleaker: six weeks of solitude in the wild. An island of my own.

Beneath the maps on the itinerary, there is a spreadsheet, listing the days of the trip alongside where I will be staying, what transport I have booked, and how I am planning to feed myself. Darwin: meals provided by the host. Stanley: bed and breakfast (food available from local stores). Bleaker: self-catering (provisions already packed in my bag, to be topped up in Stanley). Inside the little squares on the chart, the dates look small, confined and orderly. The trip does not look very long. It is not very long. It is a short jaunt, what my grandfather would have called a "jolly," and on the third page of the schedule are the words "Return Home."

The plane begins its descent into the airport, a high-fenced, khaki-coloured military base, and my stomach drops. I fold up the itinerary and tuck it back into my bag. Life is not how it looks in spreadsheets. This does not feel like a short jaunt. I am not jolly.

As I wait for my case to appear on the carousel that snakes through the small, boxy arrivals terminal, it hits me that I have never been more alone, and never further from home. The fishermen are in high spirits, talking and laughing as they shoulder their bags, present their documents to be stamped, and vanish through a door at the far end of the room. I am the last passenger remaining. After ten minutes, my case arrives, wobbling along on the conveyor belt, and for a second it looks so lonely on its precarious journey around the room that I want to cry.

Outside the terminal at Mount Pleasant, I am met by Eleanor, the owner of the guest house in Darwin where I'll spend my first nights in the Falklands. She is holding a sign that says, unpromisingly, "Mel Stevens."

In the jeep with Eleanor, I am shy and confused. She seems, in her breezy Englishness, entirely familiar—the sort of person you might run into at a farmers' market in, say, Hereford—and yet outside the car is a landscape so weird that the word I come back to over and over is *alien*. The ground is flat and beige and unchanging, a rolling scene of mud and grass and gorse. There is nothing I can see that distinguishes one mile from the next: no buildings, monuments, trees, hills. It feels as though we are at sea, surrounded by water with no sight of land, and might sink at any moment without a trace. The road cuts through space like a line across a blank page, and either side of it are wire-laced fences festooned with red signs that say "DANGER" and "MINES" under images of skulls and crossbones. The sky arching over us is the widest I've ever seen, turning pink to lilac to dark red as we drive into a blinding sunset. We are at the bottom of the world, I think. This is the bottom of the world.

Things Eleanor tells me as we drive: that she is, in fact, English, but emigrated here with her husband just after the war in 1982; that her husband is currently away competing in the Island Games, an international sporting competition for island nations that is the Falklands equivalent of the Olympics; that man-made climate change is a myth created by people who would like to see rural communities forced into cities and that if I don't believe her I should look up the mini ice-age that occurred during the reign of Henry VIII; that although she used to accept Argentinian guests at the hotel and personally has no problem with Argentinians—does, in fact, treat all nationalities equally—*some* people in the Darwin settlement found their presence disconcerting, and *some* people found their rudeness and insensitivities distressing, so she had to stop hosting them; that the only people Falkland Islanders trust less than Argentinians are writers, but that she, Eleanor, writes romantic fiction in secret.

"What do you do?" she asks, and the question hangs in the air as the sun ahead of us drops out of sight. Suddenly, it is dark, and there is nothing to puncture the blackness except for our headlights, illuminating the rubble-ridden track ahead of us and, once, the disgruntled face of a seal rolling in a stream by the road. Beyond the muddy-gold beams of the jeep, I see nothing.

"I'm a teacher," I tell her.

"What do you teach?" she asks.

"Writing."

Darwin, when we arrive, is so dark that at first I don't know why Eleanor has stopped the car. She pulls out a torch and flashes it over the settlement: three black-windowed houses, none of them apparently inhabited. One belongs to her and her husband, she says, and one to a couple who only stay during the warmer months; the last, and largest, is the hotel in which I will be the only resident. All I can make out is an impression of rows of windows with nothing behind them, and the sound of the wind sliding over the roof.

Minutes later I find myself deposited in a room in the otherwise guestless guest house, looking out from the other side of a window that now frames the expanse of blackness where I stood looking in. I hear the crunch and splatter of stones and mud under the wheels of the jeep as Eleanor drives off. I am alone.

Thoughtlessly, I pull out my phone to send a text to my family—I'm here!—but there's no phone service. There is supposed to be an Internet connection, but Eleanor, after explaining in detail a system involving scratch cards that reveal special codes, told me as she dropped me off that it wasn't working, and she had run out of cards in any case. From the window, I see the lights come on in one of the other houses: a sudden burst of electric gold that illuminates a patch of shoreline, churning water and rock. I sit on the edge of the bed and think: I am here. Time stretches ahead into the darkness. When I close my eyes I am back in the jeep on the black road, the headlight beams illuminating nothing.

Being without the Internet feels like free-floating in outer space. I cast my mind back to my childhood and early teenage years: I remember quite well how it was before the Internet became the spine of life, and yet, now, in this flat, cold, dark, empty place, not having that connection makes me feel as though I'm suffocating. I find myself horrified by the prospect of days that begin, proceed, and end in one uninterrupted whole; of the long, relentless evening ahead of me, and other evenings after that. I am appalled by the idea of missing out on the minutiae and chatter that my friends and people I used to know see fit to share online (although never before has this information seemed particularly interesting or important). I am scared that people will try to reach me with something vital, or even something fun, and I won't receive the message.

I tell myself to grow up; that this, here, is what real life is like; that this is how people lived for centuries until about five minutes ago. In a matter of days I will be in Stanley, which is, I'm sure, a citadel of cyber cafes and high-speed connections.

But still I find myself gripping the mattress, staring at the window, and feeling as though I am drifting out into the black sky untethered.

There is nothing to interrupt me here, and nothing to distract me. "Effortless concentration" seems less far-fetched at once. No Internet. No noises. Nobody passing by or updating a status or texting to suggest that we go out tonight. I am away—from my life and my friends and my family—and therefore I have arrived, suddenly and unannounced, at myself.

At nine o'clock the generator outside turns off. The comforting thrum of the machine, which I hadn't noticed until it stopped, is replaced by a shrill silence. Gradually, the heaving of waves along the shore becomes audible, and a little later, the din of my own heart. I lie in bed but can't sleep: my breath is distracting. I become aware of a constant jangling in my ears: a tinnitus too mild to notice anywhere but here.

Habits I am being forced to break:

· Wondering, "What year was so-and-so born?" or "When was such-and-such-a-thing invented?" or any other general, non-urgent but niggling question, and looking it up at once. Instead, I start a Word document listing all the things I'd google if I could: a sprawling, eclectic list of idle curiosity.
· Thinking, "I fancy Thai/Indian/Chinese food," and ordering it online.
· Thinking, "I fancy Thai/Indian/Chinese food," and texting

someone saying, "Do you want to go out for Thai/Indian/
Chinese?"
· Texting someone saying, "Do you want to go for a drink
later?" and then going for a drink later.
· Texting anyone saying anything.
· Going out for coffee.
· Going out for anything other than a windy, icy walk.

A dream: You are standing on the beach. An enormous wave
rises out of the sea. You know that you are going to be swept
away. When the wave breaks, you roll it up, the way you would a
yoga mat. You turn the crest of it over and over until your forearms ache, and you have somehow got it so tight it is solid, a bar
you can cling to. You ride it out across the ocean. Hours later,
you are washed up on a new island even more remote, somewhere in Antarctica. Here, you are greeted without surprise by
an old friend, an actor, who is waving a sabre and trying to learn
how to fence. "I've got the lunge," she tells you, demonstrating,
"but I haven't got the thrust right yet."

On my first full day in the Falklands, I walk to the world's
southernmost suspension bridge. It takes two hours to reach
from Darwin, on a muddy track littered with animal carcasses
in various stages of decomposition. En route, I pass two men,
one on a motorcycle, the other coming across the fields on a
quad bike laden with dogs. Both assume I have broken down
and left my vehicle somewhere; they offer me lifts. When I tell
one of them that I am walking "because I want to" he crows
with laughter and says, "Ye must do! Ye must do!" His accent
is something like British West Country, but every now and
then sounds both Irish and Australian. I ask how far it is to the

bridge. He says, "Oh, it's a way yet, a way yet," then laughs again and says, "No, just there in the next valley." Further on, things I expect to be people in the distance are not in fact people: an inflatable ring hanging on a pole, a windswept shrub, a gravestone.

I don't notice the noise the wind makes until I stop for a moment in the shelter of the cliffs and feel the sudden silence. The bridge, when I reach it, is horrifying. It spans the water, but panels splinter downwards and a sign nailed to a nearby post says (although the paint is so chipped it's difficult to read), "Closed to all vehicles and pedestrians." On the other side of the bay, what looks like a wrecked ship rises out of the water. Waves slap listlessly against the rocks.

It is so desolate, so isolated and so horribly quiet that I have an urge to run, but I know that wherever I run to will be the same: empty, unpopulated, full of sky and bones and water. I don't know what I am afraid of, staring at the bridge and the shipwreck and listening to the water against the shore, but I am afraid.

That night, Eleanor asks me how long I plan to stay in the Falklands. When I tell her it is nearly three months, she looks visibly shocked, and I feel the stirrings of a now-familiar panic, about how long the days, how long the weeks will be.

You Make It All Up

On my third day, Eleanor drives me from Darwin to Stanley. As we set off from the guest house in the beginnings of snow, I feel my Falklands project is really beginning.

On the way, we stop at the Argentinian cemetery: a square plot of white crosses, staked out on a hillside with nothing but a view of cloud and grey waves crashing against cliffs. The snow has turned to hail, which the wind drives in horizontally. It stings my face. The weather feels deliberately malicious.

Eleanor regards the plot through squinting eyes. "What a bleak place to end up," she says, shaking her head, and it surprises me that she has noticed how desolate it is. It doesn't strike me as particularly different from Darwin.

From the window of my new room in Stanley I see: a wide grey sky, grey water, and grey-white snow-covered land. The wind howls in off the Atlantic, pelting hail sideways into the glass. Wave after wave pounds the rocks, and splinters and churns. The horizon is cloudy, but I can still make out the silhouette of the *Lady Elizabeth,* an 1879 shipwreck that squats blackly in the water, masts erect, as though poised to attempt a return voyage. Closer by, geese waddle across the ice in front of a red, double-decker London bus, with a sign that says it's bound for Piccadilly Circus.

I will spend the next month in this guest house on the outskirts of the town, presided over by Maura, the housekeeper. Since it is the middle of winter, Maura explains, there will probably be no other guests. The owner of the hotel, Jane, is away in England. For the next few weeks, then, it will just be Maura and me.

I ask her about the Internet. "Is there Wi-Fi here?" I know, as I ask, that I sound needy, a little obsessed. I am a little obsessed.

She squints.

"Wi-Fi?" I repeat. "The Internet?"

Maura looks troubled. "The Internet?" Jane would know, she says. She leads me into the hall, and points at a bulky machine squatting on a table by the door. She looks doubtful as she says, "Is that it?"

"No," I say, "no, that's a printer."

"The Internet?" Maura repeats, again. She shrugs. "I'm sure it's around here somewhere. I'm just not sure where."

The buildings of Stanley, from the outside, all look the same, with their white walls and coloured roofs. It is only gradually that I learn to tell them apart: this one is a cafe, this is a pub, this is a store that stocks thousands and thousands of toy penguins. On the neat front lawns of the identical houses, whale vertebrae serve as garden furniture.

At the West Store, the biggest "supermarket" in town, I ask for the Internet scratch cards Eleanor mentioned. The lady at the checkout doesn't understand me, and we get stuck in a horrible loop of me repeating my request and her saying, "Eh?" Eventually she figures out what I'm looking for, repeats the phrase in her own accent, and then says something that, a beat later, I understand to be, "We've run out."

The shelves of the shop are stacked with canned and bottled goods, almost all of which are out of date. At the back is a section of "fresh" produce: battered-looking apples, wilting lettuces, dusty boxes of cherry tomatoes that cost five times what I'd expect to pay at home. Outside, a group of adults, huddled together to talk and smoke in the relative shelter of the eaves, goes silent as I pass.

I wander through the cemetery. I have to steel myself to go in. In the wind and hail-snow-sleet-rain, the boggy graves look poised to regurgitate their occupants. I move amongst them, reading names and dates. Pre-1900, the deaths are almost all early: people in their thirties or younger. There are rows of unmarked, child-sized plots, and heavy, wooden crosses, weather-worn.

Further off, a hawk is poised between headstones. It is pinning something to the ground with its leg—something grey and fluffy that from a distance looks like a rabbit. The bird takes off. Dangling from its claws: a ragged teddy bear.

If my two days in Darwin were a brief introduction to myself, to the self I am when everything else is stripped away, life in Stanley is a lesson in self-consciousness. Wherever I go, I am acutely aware of my strangeness. It is not tourist season; those cruise ships that offload hundreds of passengers in the warmer months are nowhere to be seen. I am an oddity. I am not, immediately, to be trusted.

I turn heads. I provoke scowls. I stop conversations and elicit guarded enquiries: What am I doing here? Where have I come from? What do I want? I answer these questions with varying degrees of truthfulness: I am a teacher of writing. I am from the UK, but have been living in America. I am here because . . . I want . . . I'm here to work. No, not to teach. To do my own work. I change the subject.

I don't have a desk in my room at the guest house, but I do have a dressing table. I push toiletries to one side and in their place I put my laptop. When I open it each morning it strikes me as expectant, waiting, like an impatient child, for me to tell a story. Behind it is a wall-mounted mirror that frames my reflection as I type tentative sentences and delete them, draw graphs of possible plots (X axis = time, Y axis = dramatic tension), and flick through the pages of unused notebooks as though they might contain clues.

In Darwin I was content to wander, to be occupied with settling in and looking about me. Now, in Stanley, the preamble is over and I feel increasing pressure to begin writing. The first few days, which slide by without any significant literary achievement, feel like inexcusably wasted opportunities. So: it is time to begin—to begin what? The novel I have come here to write—and what novel is that? I type, "Chapter One." I stare at the page. The cursor blinks apprehensively.

I look up from my laptop into my own frustrated face. I am battling, I know, with the incompatibility of the twin goals I set myself on this trip: to research and write the book simultaneously, to do it all at once. I don't want to start too soon, before I've really understood anything about the Falklands, or the characters I want to place here, and therefore risk setting off on the wrong track. But if I wait to start until I feel ecstatically inspired I'll be in danger of finishing nothing, never having an idea, maybe never even starting. I weigh up contradictory philosophies of creativity—Philip Pullman's "If you only write when you want to, or when you feel like it, or when it's easy, you'll always be an amateur," versus, say, Wordsworth's "Good poetry is the spontaneous overflow of powerful feelings"—and all the while look from my blank laptop to my blank reflection and back again.

It is in this state of meditative panic that it occurs to me to channel that feeling into a character: someone who is similarly paralysed by their own ambiguous ambitions, someone whose creative constipation I can laugh at and, in doing so, relieve my own. On this tentative foundation, I am able to build a person in my mind who feels real, and funny, and, as the hours at the dressing table stretch on, like surprisingly good company. I am so relieved to greet this tardy protagonist that, later that day, when Maura pokes her head around the door of my room to check on me, I forget to pretend not to be a writer and tell her I'm doing fine, because "I've finally worked out who my main character is."

Maura, standing in the kitchen over a frying pan loaded with eggs, fiddling with the buttons on her shirtsleeves: "So, you write books about people . . . ?"

"Well, yes, but not real people," I say. "I write fiction."

She looks overjoyed. Her whole face seems to relax. "Fiction! How clever! So you make it all up?"

"I do."

"That's marvellous," she says. "That's clever. That's right."

When I finally acquire a scratch card that will enable me to connect to the Internet, I get cold feet. In the days since I was last online, I have already in some ways adjusted to this quiet, disconnected life. I scrape away the silver on the back of the card with my thumbnail to reveal a string of numbers. On my computer screen, the browser opens to a window asking for the code.

I have a thought that seems irrational, but which is hard to suppress, that this might be the last happy moment of my life. I might be about to discover that something terrible has happened. The world, elsewhere, could have ended. Everyone I love could have died. More plausibly, one person I love could have died. Why this is any more likely to have happened since I've been offline than at times when I've been able to receive the news in a timely fashion is unclear—and yet. I worry.

I log on. Achingly, cringingly slowly, the BBC news page loads. George Zimmerman has been acquitted of the murder of Trayvon Martin. Edward Snowden denies that he is a Chinese secret agent. The Vatican announces that followers of the Pope's Twitter account will get time off Purgatory.

There are a few emails from my family and friends. An invitation to a party in Cambridge, Massachusetts, to celebrate the summer solstice in a few days' time. A message from my old room-mate about an outstanding electric bill we need to pay.

Everyone I love is still alive.

A Tiger on Camden High Street

am prepared. I have packed a bag with enough clothes and books to get me through the next two weeks. I have arranged to stay the night with my best friend. I have taken the following day off work in case I need time to compose myself after it's done, and I have rehearsed, meticulously, the conversation I will have with Will when he gets home. I am confident I have arranged the cleanest, most orderly break-up possible.

What I am not prepared for is that when Will arrives to find me in nervous tears on the sofa, he rushes to comfort me.

"Hey," he says. He drops his rucksack and bends over me. "Hey, what's wrong?" He tries to push my hair back from my face. He wants to look me in the eye. He strokes my head, and shoulder, and knee. "It's OK," he says. "What's wrong?"

A moment later, he notices my suitcase at the bottom of the stairs. He makes one more attempt to hold me, and when I still can't look at him, pulls away. I am too thrown by his concern, his kindness, by the staggering experience of being looked after by Will rather than looking after him, to give the speech I have prepared. Instead, I stare helplessly at the wall.

"We can work things out," he says.

We have been working things out for over two years. Ever since we graduated, I've been working a day job to pay the overpriced rent for our flat—a rickety, pretty, falling-apart loft that I love and can't really afford. After agonizing and editing and rewriting and doubt, I sent a new novel to an agent, who responded a day later saying, "I'm halfway through and I love it!" and then, the following week, "I've finished it and don't think it works." I wrote back asking to meet her, promising that I could change it, make it better; whatever she wanted me to do, I would do it. A month later, she resigned from the agency and moved to Scotland to live on a farm—her parting shot, "I found the premise fundamentally unconvincing."

I am left with Will, another novel that doesn't work, and no agent. Will is gigging with his band, a multifarious group of eccentrics with ridiculous nicknames for each other like "Dave the Bass" and "Rat." He isn't sleeping enough; he's earning too little; he's succumbing to depression and jittery anxiety—at first gradually, then all at once. Unlike others in his circle, Will refuses to self-medicate with drink or drugs, and so, for the last few months, I have been helping him to get out of bed, into the shower, to feed and dress himself. We have wide-ranging, circular discussions about whatever is consuming his mind, so that his obsessions become mine, too.

On the morning of his twenty-fifth birthday, I come downstairs to find him in his pyjamas, staring at a breakfast show on the television. It is National Anxiety and Depression Awareness Week. A Depressed Person is sitting on the sofa next to the show's host. "I would never advise anyone to have a relationship with someone suffering from depression," she is saying. "You wouldn't be a partner, you'd just be a carer."

"We can talk about this," says Will, whenever I suggest that things aren't working quite the way they should be. "I can change. I'll get better. Just tell me what to do, and I'll do it. Whatever it takes."

I feel desperately, achingly sorry for Will. More than that, I am terrified about what will happen to him when I leave. Fear has kept me here, in an intolerable stasis, until this moment. Now, what will happen to him if I leave seems less appalling than what will happen to me if I stay.

In the end he is placid about it, accepting the new terms of his life passively, as though on behalf of someone else, whom he didn't know well, or didn't care about. He sighs, sinks back into the couch and stares at his knees. His calmness makes me nauseous. I know that once I've gone, he will continue to sit there, just as he is now, and eventually he'll tap the power button on the TV remote and watch until dawn whichever channel comes on first.

To get away from him, and to delay the finality of leaving the house, I go back upstairs and gaze at our tiny bedroom, filled almost entirely with the bed, and at the study where I wrote the novel that didn't work, and at the roof terrace with its views down into gardens of people wealthier than we will ever be. A cat is winding between pot plants in the courtyard below. It strikes me that it is these things I will miss: the study and the bed and the roof terrace. They are things that have been solid and mine and reassuring. They have formed a stage set for the kind of life I thought I wanted to live.

I run back down the stairs, past Will on the sofa, and drag my suitcase out of the flat, down the stairway that runs through the building to the ground floor, and out towards the Tube station.

At first I don't notice anything strange about the street. As I cross the road, the wheels of my case catch in the gutter and it tumbles over. I have to pause to set it upright again. Gradually, I become aware of an eerie quietness, a silence that has no place in central London in the early evening, and then, as I move off again, growing gradually louder, a murmur, rumble, noise. I hear chants, shouts, breaking glass, car horns. Even when sirens are wailing and screeching in my ears, I don't fully understand that these are sounds from the real world, and not the by-products of my own confusion.

But then I turn onto the main road and fall into a mass of bodies, running, shouting. The window of a bar—a place where Will and I used to drink sometimes—has been smashed. Further off, people are throwing chairs at the front of a shop, trying to break their way in.

Someone runs into my suitcase and falls over. I turn and instinctively blurt out, "Sorry," to the teenaged boy who is sprawled on the ground. He raises his head to me—his face almost entirely obscured by a low hood—then scrambles to his feet and vanishes into the fray.

When I reach the entrance to the Tube, I find a line of police in yellow jackets staring bemusedly at the crowd, as though it is not much to do with them, as though they are watching it on the news.

"Is the station closed? I need to get into the station." I realise, as I start to speak, that I am panicking. "I need to get into the station."

The police say nothing. They don't seem to register that I am here.

"I need to get out of here," I say. "I need to get into the station. I have to get to my friend's house."

A girl younger than me, who has been jostled into the small space at my elbow, says, "Everything's closed? They won't let us through?" She looks shell-shocked. Everything she says sounds like a question. "I've been trying for ages and they won't let me through?"

"I need to leave," I say.

Finally, the police officer nearest us, whose face is inches from mine, speaks. "You should go home."

"I can't go home. I've just left home. I can't go back."

The girl turns and gazes vaguely back at the crowd. They have broken through the window of the shop, and people are shoving in and out, leaving with hands full of fizzy drinks, chocolate bars, cans of beer. A man emerges, his arms full of toilet rolls.

"I heard there's a tiger on Camden High Street," the girl says, sounding definite for the first time. "The animals have all escaped from the zoo."

The only thing worse than leaving Will is going back now, dragging my case behind me up the steps and letting myself in to find him exactly as he was before. He looks up at me with an expression of absolute hope. He thinks I've changed my mind. He thinks I've really come back.

"There's some sort of riot going on," I say as quickly as I can. "The station's closed. Holly's coming to get me in the car."

The next day, when I wake up on the futon in Holly's flat in Hackney, the whole thing seems like a fever dream: leaving Will; the riots; driving through dark, unsettlingly quiet streets, and then through crowds of people; and then hitting someone—hitting someone?—who lurched off and away without even looking back at us.

I wander downstairs to find Holly brushing her teeth in the bathroom. She is wearing a suit, about to leave for work.

"Did we run someone over last night?" I ask.

With a mouth full of toothpaste she splutters, "Technically he hit us. He kind of fell into the path of the car." A fleck of white foam lands on her lapel. "Oh, crap," she says, and scrubs at it with the inside of her wrist. She spits into the basin and turns on the tap. "He seemed more or less fine."

All the normal rules, all the things that held life together, have fallen away. I have walked out of my relationship, and my flat, and, as if in a show of solidarity, all of London has gone insane.

When, at twenty-three, I met Will at a bar, his appeal struck me as twofold. He was a scruffy, artsy-looking musician who not only wrote me witty emails that broke up my days at the office, but played keyboard in a band and offered access to a world I found appealing, intriguing, the kind of thing I'd want to write about. I liked the idea of the gigs and festivals and disappointment and success. I liked the casual, intimate friendships the bandmates had with one another; their outlandish nicknames. I liked the rusty black van that we spent a day meticulously painting with the band's name in silver, and which broke down on the way to every event.

But he was also a grown-up human male with whom I could share all the trappings of what seemed to constitute a successful life: relationship, income, home. I wanted to be a Londoner like the other Londoners I knew. I did not want to have to sacrifice any of that, just to be a writer.

It did not strike me, at first, that these two appealing features were by their very nature contradictory. And so, in my relationship with Will, I played at being the sort of person who belonged with him, just to see what it was like, but all the while I wanted it to be real, to be my life, to be solid and comfortable and genuine. I have spent two years chasing stability from an unstable man.

This premise was fundamentally unconvincing.

The radio is playing coverage of the riots: burned-down buildings, looted stores, unrest spreading to Manchester, Birmingham, Nottingham. Holly has gone, and when I turn off the news, the flat is silent. I leave and head, out of habit, to work. Outside the glass tower where I normally spend my days in front of spreadsheets and poorly written reports, I stare up towards the floor where my office is. I'm not sure why I've come here. I can't go in. Instead, I begin a ludicrous, miserable tour of the city, and spend the day crying beside famous landmarks. I call my mother in tears from the London Eye, St. James's Park, Parliament Square, and the pet emporium at Harrods.

"At first I couldn't understand why you were so upset," my mother says. "It was your decision. You've wanted to leave for so long. It was only a matter of time."

I am sitting on the steps of St. Paul's, featuring in several tourist photos of the cathedral. "I know, but—"

"But then I realized," she says, "you don't really have anything left."

I don't really have anything left: no Will, no agent, no novel.

I am about to embark on a strange period of semi-existence, though the exact details are hazy at this point. I don't know that I'm going to spend the next two months living in the Euro

Hotel at Clapham Common so I can turn up to do the job I hate and eat three meals a day at Pret a Manger. I don't know that I'll move from there to a flat on a council estate in Deptford where the local children will inexplicably nickname me "Princess Diana" and heckle me every time I walk to the bus stop. I don't know that, in mid-December, my boss will summon me to suggest I focus more on admin and let my male assistant tackle the editorial side of things, nor that this will prompt me to quit in a rage and later turn up drunk and belligerent at the office Christmas party.

I don't really have anything left. I am not so much back to square one as knocked completely off the board.

A woman approaches me, climbing the steps in twos, holding a camera. "Could you move to the left a bit?" she asks, breathless. "I'm trying to take a picture and you're in the way."

Bleaker House: SITUATION

How many hours of his life had he spent in the Bodleian Library? Ollie wondered if the time could be added up, like those stories people told: by the time you die, you'll have spent five years on the toilet, thirty sleeping, three brushing your teeth, four having sex. How many years would he spend having sex? And how many, sitting, as he was now, in the Upper Reading Room of the Bodleian Library at Oxford University, staring at but not reading pages from Ian Watt's *The Rise of the Novel* and listening to the slap and shuffle of the librarian's shoes as she paced across the uneven wooden floor?

That morning, he had defended his DPhil thesis in front of a pair of experts in eighteenth-century fictions of masculinity. They had listened with frowns of varying severity as he presented an argument about capitalism, the division of labour and the fracturing of the patriarchal ideal. It had been going quite well, he thought—the brows of his examiners had been only lightly creased—and then, mid-sentence, he had fallen apart. He had been saying something about time, about a new narrative sense of chronology and causality evidenced by the writing of . . . of who? He remembered nothing. He had no ideas. His thesis, sitting neatly bound on the table between hands he knew were his own, looked like a dull book by a stranger; something he hadn't got around to reading yet. There was simply no way, after that, that they could pronounce him a Doctor of Philosophy.

The summer ahead was a blank—a cloud of unstructured time hovering above him. The thought of staying in the library, of revising and resubmitting the thesis, was oppressive. But if not that, then what else could he do?

The next day, in the dawn quiet of the flat he shared with his girlfriend, Mei, the library and the viva seemed both distant and relentlessly present in his mind.

Clutching the post and a cup of tea, he slid out onto the small patch of paving behind the flat that Mei called the back yard, and sat on the step. It was light, but getting warm already. By his feet, terracotta pots held dead shrubs that Mei had planted and briefly nurtured before losing interest. Their crisp leaves rustled in the breeze; around their stalks, cigarette stubs were crushed into the soil.

He had slept badly. His dreams had transported him back to the room where his viva had been held, in which he had experienced a variety of surreal humiliations: giving a lecture naked, performing a play without knowing his lines, attempting to explain the argument of his second chapter to a panel of examiners who all had Mei's face and who cut him short to explain that they were leaving him for someone called "the Professor."

Ollie shuddered and turned his attention to the post in his

lap. He sifted through the pile: letters from the bank, a leaflet from the Liberal Democrats, a newsletter from his college, several things addressed to the flat's previous occupants who hadn't lived there for years, and then, at the bottom, a dog-eared letter with Ollie's name and address handwritten in black ink. Its stamp depicted two penguins balancing on a block of ice, and was labelled, "Falkland Islands." Holding it closer to his face, he inhaled something pungent that immediately brought to mind images of mud, cows, fertilizer.

He turned the letter over. When he slid a finger under the envelope's flap, it crackled as though it had been sealed for years.

Dear Oliver Newman,

This is a letter from your FREND in the FALKLAND ISLANDS. I have informacean to offer regarding your father ALSOP GRAVES, who you believe to be diseased. Please visit me imeadiatly to make arangments for the colection of the urgent informacean regarding your FATHER. You will have to take an airaplain to get here. The airaplain arrives every Saturday. TIME is short so hurry. I will expect you on Saturday. TIME is short.

Regards, a letter and an offer of informacean from,
Your FREND in the FALKLAND ISLANDS.

Bleaker Island
The Falkland Islands
South Atlantic

A Stringent Anti-Five-O'Clock-Tea Law

Whenever Maura is home, the radio is on. It plays a vital role, here, where the Internet is unreliable, and televised news is distributed weekly on a DVD. The first time I listen, the DJs are playing a game called "Guess Who?": islanders call in and the hosts have to guess who they are from their voices alone. Sometimes, the wind blows so loudly outside that I have to turn up the volume to hear the weather forecast (it's windy, the DJ says, and snowing) over the roar and bluster.

Now that Ollie has arrived, the shape of my novel unspools as I work at the dressing table. By the end of my second week, I have plotted the bulk of it out, sketching the overall arc of the narrative under section headings: Situation, Complication, Climax, Resolution. These categories are comforting, even the ones that are, at this point, still empty in my mind: they evoke the reassurance of textbooks, and the memory of a student I taught while studying for my MFA in Boston who surveyed the same chalked words on the blackboard with a look of surprised relief and said, "Oh, so it's kind of like painting by numbers?"

Ollie is a PhD student who grew up in Oxford and at twenty-five is surprised, embarrassed and yet simultaneously relieved to find that he has somehow never moved away from the city of his birth. I know people like this. I grew up with people like this. If one or two things about my life had worked out differently perhaps I would be like this, and my starting point for the character—that awkward, anxious, guilty sense of underachievement—feels as central to my own nature as it is to his. Ollie is sheltered, nervous, pointlessly intelligent, ambitious within narrow confines. The world he occupies is the dusty, hushed Bodleian Library, the loneliness of research, the intimacy of knowing great literature very well, the frustrations of knowing little else.

Ollie has been raised by his mother to believe that his father, who she met when he was visiting England from the Falkland Islands, died a week after she met him. The novel opens with a letter arriving at Ollie's shabby student flat. Ollie's father is not dead, the anonymous writer says; Ollie should know the truth, and he should come to the Falklands to discover it.

I take Ollie out of Oxford and I put him in the Falklands: first I take him to Stanley, like me, and then both of us will travel onwards to Bleaker Island. The incongruity between his tame, obdurate persona and the weirdness of his new surroundings is supposed to be funny. The whole set-up is supposed to be funny. It is so nonsensical for someone like Ollie, and for someone like me, to be where we are that the reasoning behind it can't help but seem far-fetched. *I want to write a novel. I am looking for my father.*

. . .

In Stanley's government archives, I search for stories I could incorporate into Ollie's, but it is Annabel, the archivist, who yields the most telling information.

"They did a family-tree project at the primary school," she says, "and found out that every single child was related. So now I keep tabs on it in a database. In case anyone falls in love with the wrong person." She pats a large, whirring computer monitor on her desk. "Sometimes the families are so mixed up with each other that the program asks me if I'm really sure about the data," she adds.

I leaf through copies of *Falkland Islands Magazine* from the 1890s, which is a catalogue of unusual ways to die: shot in the head when embracing a friend out hunting; over-exposure while stuck in a peat bog; entangled in kelp while swimming away from a shipwreck; trapped on a boat crushed between two icebergs. And drowning after drowning after drowning. People kept falling off cliffs in the dark.

February 1891. On the health of the Falkland Islanders: "Never was there such a race of dyspeptic mortals. . . . The causes are said to be the fondness of the islanders for strong tea and coffee, which they consume in vast quantities. . . . The remedy is obvious. The Governor must get a stringent anti-five-o'clock-tea law passed."

There is so much weather here that sometimes it can be several things at once. When I reach the guest house after a day in the archives, the sun is setting over the bay, sending streaks of yellow and red into a crisp blue sky to the west. Overhead, hailstones are plummeting from a thunderous grey cloud like seeds being sown, and an angry wind is picking them up and hurling them sidelong against the windowpane.

· · ·

In the West Store, teenage girls are shoplifting make-up. They wear hoodies that say "British & Fabulous," which they must have ordered from a catalogue. "It's easy," one of them whispers. "No one's looking. No one cares." Outside, seagulls hover over the road, dropping mussels from a height to break the shells.

On the Other Side

At the edge of Stanley, there is a cattle grid. It marks a boundary: on one side is the town, and on the other is "camp," a term that covers every part of the Falklands that is not Stanley. This cattle grid is the site of frequent car crashes. There are three reasons for this.

First: Maura explains that after the war, when they built the road that led out of town, there were instructions for a drainage ditch on either side. An overenthusiastic digging team mistook the annual rainfall figure for the monthly one, and created deep, gaping ditches into which cars now slide off the icy road.

Second: There is no cinema, no theatre, no evening entertainment in Stanley, but there are seven pubs. As everyone I meet wants to tell me, "It's a drinking culture, here." By ten o'clock most nights, everyone is exceedingly drunk. Then they get into their Land Rovers and drive home.

Third: It is against the law to drive drunk in Stanley, but

legal in camp. Drunk drivers who have caught the attention of the police are routinely pursued through town until they reach the grid, at which point the chase ends and the fleeing driver hurtles across and straight into the ditch. When I express a degree of surprise that people so frequently risk their lives in this manner, Maura shrugs and says, "If you're going to crash your car blind drunk, it's better to do it on the other side."

Spies

As time passes in Stanley, I begin to feel I am failing at my mother's directive to "meet some *people*." I have been here for a fortnight and, other than Maura, and Annabel in the archives, have not exactly made any friends.

Over breakfast, Maura tells me stories about her early life, when she kept cows on West Falkland and put milk in the well to keep it cool; when she made butter by hand and pickled it in winter; when she carried her babies around in panniers across the back of her horse. She talks in a low, agitated voice about the arrival of Argentinian soldiers in her house, how they pointed their guns at her son and "spoke foreign" to her, and how she had never felt the same way about strangers after that. But before the war, before the tracks and roads were built, she used to ride between settlements, she says, "and everyone was pleased to see you. Not like now when people are always suspicious. Even if they'd never seen you before, in the old days, you were treated like a friend."

It is time, I decide, to meet some people, and the place to meet them, Maura says, is in the pub. "Go to the Globe. People will tell you stories in the Globe."

It is odd to me that I feel adventurous enough to travel half-way around the world by myself, but terrified by the prospect of walking, alone, into a pub on a Friday night. But Maura has made it clear, first in hints and then overtly, that it is considered unacceptable, rude, to stay in Stanley without doing this; I brace myself to make my debut.

The Globe bar looks like all the other whitewashed shacks in Stanley from the outside, but inside it is a high-ceilinged, open space that feels as though it has been perfectly preserved from decades ago. Flags cover the rafters. Tables and chairs are strewn haphazardly across the floor. Surfaces are a disconcerting combination of dusty and sticky. There's no white wine. There's no rosé. I order red.

When I arrive, around nine p.m., it is quiet. There are a couple of men playing pool, and a drunken group of women at the bar. One of them turns as I sit down in a corner; she stares blearily, as though she can't quite focus, then shouts, "Excuse you!" I don't know what it is that I'm being excused for, and worry I have unwittingly committed a Falklands faux pas. Perhaps I have taken a seat reserved for a particularly venerated regular, and news of this transgression is going to spread around town. I switch to a different table, just to be sure.

An elderly woman is sitting by herself and saying, to nobody in particular, "It's my birthday. Will you buy me a drink? It's my birthday." When I go back to the bar to get her something, the man serving me says, "It's not her birthday," but by that point I've already paid.

I sit alone for about an hour, working through successive glasses of dust-flecked red wine that go straight to my head but nonetheless fail to stifle my self-consciousness. And then I look up to find that the place is, suddenly, full of boys. They look like high-school students to me, and I am certain they are all under-age. A few moments later I hear their voices and realize they are British, and a beat or so after that I realize they aren't in fact children at all. They are soldiers.

The locals in the Globe exhibit an avuncular fondness for them, smiling indulgently as the young men drink and shout. They fill every corner of the room, including mine, and slur their words as they ask me, several times over, what I'm doing there all by myself. This is their night off, they say. They have come from the military base at Mount Pleasant, and will be heading back there first thing in the morning; tonight they are crashing at the barracks in town and are taking the oppor-tunity to drink as much as they possibly can. To deflect their bemused questions—What brought me here? How long have I been here? Why?—I ask them about themselves. A tall Scottish squaddie slides heavily into the chair beside me and knocks the table with his knees so that all the drinks sway in their glasses.

"In Afghanistan, I shot a fourteen-year-old boy in the chest," he says. "It opened him right up." He makes a gesture with his hands bursting out from his heart as though he were releasing a dove.

I don't know whether he's telling the truth, a macabre lie, or something in between.

"Was that the first time you shot someone?" I ask.

He shakes his head. "First time, there was this old man with a stick hobbling up to the checkpoint. They're not supposed to approach the checkpoint and he doesn't stop when we fire warning shots, and it's my job to kill him if he keeps on walking. But I panic and I shoot him in the leg instead. So we take him in, patch him up, and he tells us that Allah came to him in a dream and ordered him to commit suicide by walking to the checkpoint. "Anytime you want to try that again," I tell him, "you're welcome. Come on down. Just try it." Before we sent him packing the guys took his walking stick off him. Later they gave it back to me in a frame as a memento."

"They framed his walking stick?"

"Shall I come back with you to your place?" the soldier asks.

"No," I say. "That's OK." I put on my coat and blurrily check that I have my purse.

He looks nonplussed at my departure, and helps himself to my unfinished wine. "Goodnight, wee woman," he says.

Though I am strange in Stanley, to the locals and increasingly to myself, it turns out that I am not in fact the only oddball who has washed up on the islands in search of something. A few days after my excursion to the Globe, I learn that there is another foreigner in town. I spot him walking up and down the waterfront, taking selfies in front of the church, the whale-bone arch, the governor's house. The first time he speaks to me, it is to ask me to photograph him next to a flock of upland geese. As I line up the shot, he tells me, in a rush of over-enunciated words, that he is an American currently living in Japan, a linguist, an expert in pronunciation and dialect. He has come to the Falklands to study speech patterns, but nobody will speak to him.

He pulls out his iPhone and shows me an app he has created, designed to teach Japanese people to speak English in a variety of accents. The options are: America, America (Southern), Canada, England, England (Northern), Scotland, Wales, Australia, New Zealand, South Africa. He wants to add the Falklands accent to his collection, but first, he needs to master it himself. He needs people to speak to him.

He looks me in the eye as though he suspects I don't believe him and says, "How are you? My name is Tony!" in each of the accents offered on the app, with the panache of a magician performing a trick. He expects me to be amazed. For the most part, he is unconvincing. The attempt at Welsh is particularly bad. He is unable to confirm, when I ask, whether there is much demand in Japan for tuition in speaking English with a Falklands accent.

It's freezing on the waterfront. The spattering of rain is solidifying into hail. I interrupt Tony long enough to gesture at the weather as an excuse to leave, and hurry away. As I jog back home, bent into the wind, I figure that he is an eccentric, a little unhinged, a little weird, essentially harmless.

A couple of days later, I am sitting in a large leather armchair in the sitting room of the guest house, reading, when I overhear a conversation between Maura and Paola, the Chilean woman who does the cleaning. They don't seem to know I am here; the back of the chair is hiding me from view. They are talking about Tony.

"He is a shady character for sure," Maura is saying, "coming here, asking questions."

A murmured assent from Paola.

Maura goes on: "His stories don't add up, you know."

"They don't," says Paola.

Maura: "Everyone is saying so. When he first comes up to me, in the West Store, he said he was on holiday. Then he made a slip though, didn't he, and said he was working. What kind of work is he doing that he wants to lie about like that?"

Paola makes a noise that suggests there can be no innocent answer.

"Now he says he wants to talk to people. Wants to come in here and ask me questions. What does he want to go asking people questions for? He looks like an Argentinian. He says he lives in Japan but he looks like an Argentinian, doesn't he?"

"He looks like an Argentinian," Paola confirms. "And I hear him speaking Spanish on the telephone."

"There you are," says Maura. "He's an Argentinian. Asking questions. He's a journalist. He's writing about us all."

This overheard outpouring of suspicion, assumption, guesswork and paranoia is the result of an entrenched, long-held, Falklands-wide belief that foreigners who come in and ask questions are bad news. The connections Maura makes between stranger and Argentinian and journalist are almost seamless. There have been journalists, she says, who came and asked questions and then twisted the answers they were given to make the islanders seem backward, or racist, or stupid. Being a journalist in Stanley is tantamount to being a spy.

I sink down into the chair and wonder whether they say this kind of thing about me, too. When I say I am a "teacher of writing," what is it that they think? Is the fact that I have tried to disguise my work, that I have been vague about what it is I'm doing, used against me as evidence of my untrustworthiness? When Maura looks in on me typing away at the dressing table, is she feeling the same dread and hostility that fills her voice as she talks about Tony? For a second, I find myself looking forward to leaving for Bleaker: being entirely alone seems preferable, now, to being surrounded by people who don't like you.

Am I as unsettling to Maura as the American/Japanese/Argentinian linguist?

I think—I hope—not. The fact that I am relatively young, and female, helps. It makes me appear less of a threat. I have heard people refer to me as "the young girl"; Maura bustles into the house each morning with the question, "How's my little one today?"

But I do feel awkward, sitting there in the big leather chair, listening to the two women accuse the eccentric linguist of spying and *writing about them*; because of course it is me who is spying, if only accidentally, and it is me who is writing about them.

You're looking the wrong way, I think. You've got the wrong guy.

Alternative Openings

WARNING: Although this area is believed to be clear of mines, it is possible that a mine may be washed ashore from a nearby minefield.

s this cabin fever? After three weeks in Stanley, I am suddenly full of ennui. I feel caged, antsy, checking the table of dates on my itinerary and wondering, over and over, *how many more days?* The answer is, of course, *many more days*, and that I need to stop counting and keep working. But in this restless, gloomy mood, time seems to have stuttered to a slow, sick crawl.

I know I cannot afford to be so precious. I have to be strict with myself. Read. Take vitamin D in an attempt to compensate for the dismal lack of sunlight. Go for walks (oh, but the walks, the walks, the flat, miserable countryside, with nothing to vary it but the occasional skull-and-crossbones landmine sign and the churn of the Atlantic beyond the scrubby coast). And write. Push your brain. Work.

I get no texts, no calls. My phone no longer buzzes with emails. In the uninterrupted hours, I become aware of my moods changing almost by the minute, and surrounded by the frozen silence of the rest of the day, these shifts feel monumental. To counteract this, I devise ways to interrupt myself. I set arbitrary alarms. At 14:45, I tell myself, I'll stop working and go for a run. At 17:09, I'll make coffee.

Bleaker House: SITUATION

Ollie's mother met his father at a farmers' market in Oxford. His father had looked lost, she said, wandering aimlessly, clutching a potato he didn't seem to know how to pay for. He had been in the country a few days, and was bemused by it. He knew how nothing worked: buses, streetlights, automatic doors and credit cards were all miraculous and threatening to him.

The way Ollie's mother told it, the attraction was mutual and instant—his father was wild looking and strong, and before long they were exchanging life stories. He told her tall tales of the Falklands: of storms and waves as high as houses; of a sheep that gave birth to conjoined lambs, one black, one white, both writhing, wet, twitching their shared leg as though to free themselves. He described elephant seals dragging their bulk from the sea and screaming like babies; albatrosses lifting a live foal from its mother's teat; a beached whale dying loudly and pungently, pounding the sand with its tail. He told her how soldiers had arrived on orange boats, jabbering in Spanish, shivering, gesticulating with dripping guns, how he had let his prize bull loose on them and how they had fled in fear, and all the while Ollie's mother, who was twenty years old and had never left Oxfordshire, listened and nodded and told him to go on. She was, she reported, putty in his rough, gnarled hands.

Within days of their first meeting, Ollie had been conceived. And within a week, his mother said, waving a hand as though this were an inconsequential detail, his father had, you know, died in a freak accident with a toaster.

My writing sessions at the dressing table become fitful and disjointed in this mood. I take run-ups at the beginning, trying it from several different angles. I cast my line, over and over, into the water, waiting for something to bite.

In front of me, my reflection is scowling in the mirror, sulky lower lip protruding. I exaggerate the frown and stick my tongue out. It's just a story. Just words in one order or another. It's supposed to be fun.

I meet my own eye and then blink, in the hope that this might dismiss the petulant, self-pitying thoughts that are almost obscuring the novel from view.

Bleaker House: SITUATION

Alsop Graves was a master of fucking. The English girl was under him, sweating and moaning and urging him on. They had barely left the bedroom in a week.

He bellowed as he came, then rolled off her, wiping his mouth with the back of his hand. As he sank back onto sheets patterned with roses and stared at the low, white ceiling overhead, he felt his body tingling with confidence. He was still the same Alsop Graves in England as he was at home. He could still impress and dominate and feel masterly; he was still a hero. His future, his new life in this foreign land, stretched ahead of him full of glorious possibility.

A short while later, the girl went out to buy milk and suggested Alsop make toast, gesturing at a small, boxy contraption on the kitchen counter. Alsop applied himself to the task with full attention, peeling apart bread someone had already cut, compressing the lever and scrutinizing the machine's hellish interior glow. It smelled at once familiar—the stove in the Graveses' house burning early in the morning, his mother leaning the weight of her body onto the knife as she sliced a loaf, the suggestion of warmth—and unnerving. It emitted a strange, unearthly hum. Alsop waited and imagined the return of the English girl, how he would present her with the peculiar, mechanical toast. They would eat it together and afterwards do again what they had already done so many times upstairs on the floral sheets. In a week or so, or a month or so, they'd marry. He'd buy a farm.

He prodded the appliance with a knife the way he might stoke a fire at home, and when the electric current shot through the metal into his body, his only feeling was of anticipation.

A Very Short Employment History

am having difficulty breathing. It starts about three
months into my first real job.

I have graduated from university and moved to London.
I have a place to live and a cat. I work for a human-rights organization, which strikes me as, if not interesting in the day-to-
day sense, at least an interesting thing to tell people at parties.
I am pleased to be doing something that sounds significant
and adult, and since it is 2009, in the midst of the recession,
I'm lucky to have a job at all. But, still, I am having difficulty
breathing.

One morning I come into work to find four photographs of
a woman being stoned to death on my desk. She is buried up to
her neck. The side of her head is bleeding. Her mouth is wide
open and you can tell she is wailing. Someone has stuck a yellow
Post-it note onto the last image: "Press Release!!!"

A doctor listens to my symptoms—shortness of breath, a

feeling that I can't fill my lungs, compulsive yawning, occasional panic—and prescribes Valium. I spend a week floating through work on a gentle, sunny high, writing press releases about torture, harassment of lawyers and arbitrary detention with giggly flourishes. Then I decide that clear-headed panic is preferable to vapid fuzziness and dump the pills.

I write fiction in the bodies of emails and spreadsheets so that anyone passing my screen will think I'm working. When I get home I have to decipher charts and disconnected paragraphs in which figures and budgets are dispersed between lines of a novel about an amateur Van Gogh scholar who is dying of lung cancer.

EXPENSES SHEET NAME 1-RCP-U064		
4th Dec 2009	French Translator fees	GBP 1345:70
	When I close my eyes, what I see is an image of my own lungs. They loom. They seem, after a while, not like lungs so much as wings, hovering across the retina, about to flap: it leads me to thinking of Van Gogh again, of how he wrote, once, to his brother Theo, "Oh, give me the freedom to be a bird like other birds." They flap, my lungs; they wish to be lungs like other lungs. What the doctor was saying about cell growth, metastasis, loved	

	ones, carcinoma, was a distraction from this new weight. I tried to listen to him; he was very kind—a man with a serious face and sad eyes—but in the end I wished he would be quiet so that I could concentrate. He was saying something about tying up loose ends; I think that was the phrase he used. I wanted a moment to feel my way around this new chest of mine. The x-ray image, which I still see now, of that white shadow clinging like a spider to the left lung—astonishing that something so small could be so deadly—they called that white thing cancer but I feel that is not true. They say that I am dying but it feels to me that I have realized a loss.	
29th Jan 2010	Event assistance inc. tech and catering	GBP 3250
9th March 2010	Cash Advance for Farsi translator	GBP 200:35

Somewhere in the world, someone does something terrible. Someone else reports it to their government, or to an NGO, or to a journalist, and the news eventually travels to a minor human-rights organization in London, where, before long, it arrives on my desk. I write a press release about it. The next day, somewhere else in the world, or in the same place, someone else or the same person does some other terrible thing. I write a press release about that, too. It strikes me that the day people stop doing terrible things, I'll be out of a job.

EXPENSES SHEET NAME 1-RCP-U067		
10th Aug 2010	Arabic Translator fees	GBP 525
	We talk about death so much, I realize; my head is full of little puns I am dying to share. I know, really, that these are not as funny as they seem to me and I am glad the only person I can inflict them on is myself. *This will be the death of me. No need to look so grave. Oh, stop it, stop it, really, you're killing me.* Sometimes I am amazed to be myself—sixty-one years old, not looking so bad for all those years, and just beginning to touch on the point in life where people will laugh at my jokes rather than roll their eyes and change the topic of conversation. *There's a problem with my lungs: I can't stop coffin.* I have begun to be more lenient with	

	myself recently, letting myself do things that are perhaps a little eccentric, things that I once would have resisted: chuckling at jokes I tell myself in my head, whistling the tune blasted from the windows of a passing car long after it has gone, smiling at anyone beautiful on the Tube. I am only just beginning to notice how beautiful people on the Tube are.	
16th Aug 2010	Print expenses for Brazil report	GBP 4015:77

What should a writer do, if she can't support herself by writing? I am a jumble of aspirations and overlapping motivations: I want to have a normal job, to live in the real world, to get on the train every morning and go to the pub after work, because that is what life is like, and I want to know all about life. I am twenty-three and I am learning what it is to work. If I won the lottery right now, I tell myself, I wouldn't quit, because how could anyone write from outside the realm of normal existence, of commuting and leaves on the line and birthday cake in the third-floor kitchen and departmental meetings in which people use *action* and *impact* as verbs? And besides, I have not won the lottery. I don't even buy tickets. The value of showing up at the office each morning is therefore not up for debate: I have rent to pay; I have a living to make.

And—but?—I have stories to write.

. . .

Approach One: The writer takes a job that contrasts with her literary work, that uses entirely different mental and/or physical muscles. She becomes a builder, landscape gardener, personal trainer, postal worker, traffic warden. When her formal working day is done, the writer sits down at her desk and finds her creative faculties replete, untouched, raring to go. Examples of Approach One: James Kelman, bus driver; T. S. Eliot, bank clerk; William S. Burroughs, exterminator.

Approach Two: The writer is employed in an area related to writing. She works in education, publishing, theatre, advertising, and hopes that the content of her days will filter into the content of her books, that the skills practised, lessons learned and contacts made at work will enable her to further her own alternative career. Examples of Approach Two: F. Scott Fitzgerald, copywriter; Robert Frost, English teacher; Toni Morrison, editor.

The human-rights job is, I think, an attempt at Approach Two, which I am now histrionically resenting for not being more like Approach One. The result: chronic shortness of breath, a disjointed, piecemeal novel and a string of decidedly lacklustre appraisals from my boss.

After a year in human rights, I attempt a transition towards Approach One by applying for a position in event management that is only four days a week. Despite my best efforts to explain the logic of my decision to end my human-rights career, the email circulated to all staff by the office manager reads, "Nell Stevens is taking an early retirement."

When I start my new job, Mondays are for writing. Every other day is a blur of photocopying and name-badge printing and travel bookings and canapé orders. It also becomes apparent that while Mondays are, technically, my day off, I'm still expected to be available by email and phone, and so they are better classified as working-from-home days. I set myself up in the little study at the top of the North London flat that I now share with Will, and then spend the day staring obsessively at my mobile, dreading the moment when it rings.

When the director asks me to run a series of conferences in Hong Kong, which will mean being away for weeks on end, I agree, partly because I've never been to Hong Kong, partly because it will be time away from Will, who by now has begun his descent into listless depression, and partly because it will give me an excuse not to come into the office.

The subject of the conferences I will be running is "Suicide Prevention in Asian Cities." Years later, when I put this detail into a short story called "The Personal Assistant," for a fiction workshop at BU, Leslie says I should replace it with something less far-fetched. "I just don't believe that job exists," he says. "Come up with something normal—something someone would actually do."

In Hong Kong I am so solitary and disorientated that I develop a relationship with Google. I type the beginnings of questions into the browser. It finishes them for me by supplying the concerns of other people. It is almost like having a conversation with someone:

Is it stupid to—
Is it stupid to buy a new car
Is it stupid to quit my job
Is it stupid to wear boots in summer
Is it stupid to wear fake glasses

. . .

My phone rings. A man wants to speak to Neil Stevens.

"I think you must mean me. Nell. Nell Stevens."

"No," he says, "no. I want to speak to your husband, Neil."

Thirty floors below my hotel window, cars are streaming along the road in bands of white and red. Light floods up the sides of the buildings: advertisements that coat the city in a permanent glow that feels almost audible. There's a balcony on the other side of the glass, but the door to it has been sealed for years, ever since a local singer jumped from one of the adjacent rooms and fell twenty-four floors to his death. The man on the phone hangs up.

> Is it stupid to believe in god
> Is it stupid to get back with your ex
> Is it stupid to get a tattoo in another language

The only thing that really changes in Hong Kong is that now I can hyperventilate on the thirtieth floor of buildings instead of the third. Approach One is not working out any better than Approach Two. At this point it seems necessary to admit that the problem is not with the approaches. The problem must be with me.

I turn, again, to Google and search for "Creative Writing MFA programmes with financial aid."

> How can I—
> How can I make money
> How can I lose weight
> How can I keep from singing
> How can I stop snoring

How can I help Gaza
How can I stop sweating
How can I be happy
How can I tell which ipad I have

SEMINAR SERIES 9 EXPENSES		
18th Feb 2011	Catering	GBP 305:10
	My name is Anthony Long. I tell this to myself. I am dying and I feel that I have lost something. I am dying. I test those three words out as I would chords for a new composition. I have made a career out of composing music and you have probably, without knowing it, heard some of my work: I wrote the jingle for an advert for hay-fever medicine; that is probably the best-known thing. I have lived in London my whole life, was married to a woman for ten years; I think I am a cat person but have only ever kept dogs. I have become a man who laughs to himself at bus stops, and it seems, now, more important than ever to say these	

	things, if only to myself. *Please give me the freedom to be a bird like other birds.*	
11th March 2011	Event assistance plus tech support	GBP 1012:50

A Perfect Formula

n early scenes of Ryan Murphy's film adaptation of Elizabeth Gilbert's *Eat Pray Love*, Julia Roberts gets up in the middle of the night and prays to God to tell her what to do. She is unhappily married and wants to travel the world. Her husband doesn't understand her. She is stifled by her successful life in New York. On her knees, she clasps her hands together so tightly her knuckles turn white. She says, *Hello, God . . . nice to finally meet you. I'm sorry I've never spoken directly to you before, but I hope I've expressed my ample gratitude for all the blessings you've given* [pause] *to me in my life.*

I know every single word of this scene by heart.

I know this not because I am a fan of Julia Roberts, or Ryan Murphy, or Elizabeth Gilbert. Rather, it's because *Eat Pray Love* is the only film I watch in the Falklands.

I didn't plan to spend my fellowship studying, intensely, the story of "one woman's search for everything," but before I left home, I was incapable of imagining a world without Netflix, and so didn't think to prepare a supply of entertainment. *Eat Pray Love* happens, by complete coincidence, to be the only film I have on my computer—a lightweight laptop with no DVD drive. The idea that there would be no way to stream video in the Falklands did not cross my mind before I left—let alone the thought of no high-speed Wi-Fi, let alone the spluttering, extortionate Internet connection that only works 10 per cent of the time, and even then, barely manages to load text-only emails, or the topmost slice of a digital photograph.

When I realize my mistake, I panic. I make plaintive calls to my family, and send pleas to friends for suggestions. In Stanley there are places I can buy DVDs, but without a way to play them on my computer, they'll be useless on Bleaker. I investigate the option of ordering a DVD drive online, but delivery to the Falklands would take weeks; not even Amazon can get to this remote corner of the South Atlantic in time. I optimistically buy *The Graduate* from iTunes, and get through scratch card after scratch card of Internet time before giving up, the film 2.3 per cent downloaded, an estimated eighty-nine hours remaining until completion.

This is frustrating because I know it should not be as troubling to me as it is. I did not travel to the bottom of the world to watch films. I did not travel to the bottom of the world to spend a lot of time and money trying to acquire films to watch. I came here to write, and should therefore accept that for the duration of my stay on Bleaker Island, if I *don't* want to write (or read, or sleep, or venture out for a walk in sub-zero temperatures along the shoreline), the thing I will be doing is watching *Eat Pray Love*.

"It's the only film I have with me," I tell Annabel, the archivist, a few days before I am due to leave for Bleaker.

"That's wonderful," she says. "It's a perfect formula. You can write your own version."

There's a man in the archive reading room who is trying to research his family history. He has flown to Stanley from an island off West Falkland specifically for this task, and is filling the room with a distinctly agricultural smell. He looks up now in a way that suggests he'd prefer silence, but Annabel overrules him. She is familiar, it turns out, with the film's plot. She wants to help me craft a kind of sequel.

"Make sure you've left someone behind who is heartbroken over you," she says, "but tell him this is something you just *have to do—for your art*. Then, now, in Stanley, you're in the eating phase. You have to stuff yourself for the next few days."

I consider Stanley's gastronomic offerings. Cans of out-of-date soup. UHT milk. Bread that arrives already mouldy. Everything is shipped around the world from England, except for the "fresh" produce, which comes battered and withered after a sea journey from Chile. I paid six pounds for a saggy, sad lettuce, before learning to do as the locals do: stick to vitamin tablets and artificial-fibre gel.

"What about on Bleaker Island?" I ask.

"You have to have a spiritual awakening. Wander around and pray in splendid isolation. Makes perfect sense."

"What about the love part?"

Annabel stalls. I tell her I have a one-night layover in Santiago airport on my way home and she says, "Well then, there you go. In Santiago, you have to *get it on*."

[Gasping. Tears.] *I'm in serious trouble. I don't know what to do. I need an answer. Please. Tell me what to do. Oh God, help me please.* [Tears.] *Tell me what to do and I'll do it.* [Pause, then, in a different tone of voice.] *Go back to bed, Liz.*

I would like to say that I don't know why I have *Eat Pray Love* on my computer, but the truth is that I have a weakness for saccharine Hollywood films in which women with nice hair and no cellulite get all they want at the end, as long as all they want is a husband. This predilection has overridden my strong dislike of anything that resembles "self help," which *Eat Pray Love* most definitely does.

That said, if I were given the chance to choose, consciously, a film to watch repeatedly for weeks on end, I like to think I'd pick something less embarrassing.

Maura's prediction that I would be the only guest at the house during my stay in Stanley turns out to be incorrect. On the day before I am due to leave for Bleaker, a Swiss ornithologist arrives. He is staying a few nights only, then heading to a small, outlying island to the west to study the migratory behaviour of caracaras.

I am back in the large leather chair in the sitting room, reading again, when for a second time I overhear a conversation I'm not supposed to. The ornithologist is with Maura, asking her about thermal clothing, local birdlife experts, and some kind of radio equipment he is trying to track down in Stanley. I suddenly feel horribly underprepared for Bleaker. I have been in a state of anxious denial about my imminent departure.

"Who's the girl who's staying here?" the ornithologist asks.

So this is it, I think. This is when I find out what Maura thinks of me. I recall the bitter, defensive way she talked about Tony the linguist: a shady character, a spy.

"Oh, Nell?" says Maura. "She's a young American authoress. She's here writing a history of the islands. She works at the archives, but she spends most of her time playing on her Game Boy. Anyhow, she's leaving for Bleaker Island tomorrow."

I am amazed by this report, and it takes me a little while to make sense of it. This is what Maura has supplied to fill the gaps I have intentionally left in my accounts of myself. I would have thought the conversation she and I had about my work being fiction, about making things up, would have stayed in her mind, but considering how much time I have spent with Annabel in the archives, it is reasonable enough for her to think I'm working on a history book. "American" is surprising, but perhaps understandable since the fellowship paying for my trip is from Boston University, and my T's sometimes sound with an American flatness that I struggle and fail to correct. The Game Boy, though, is the real mystery. A few minutes later, when the conversation has moved back to caracaras, I look down at the Kindle in my hands and realize the source of the confusion.

Later that night, I sit on the floor of my bedroom counting raisins. I have planned carefully for this moment. I have brought supplies with me from England, topped them up from the limited offerings of the West Store, and am now attempting final calculations. The strict baggage limit for the tiny red planes that transport people around the Falklands restricts how much food I can bring with me to the island. At Stanley airport, I will be weighed alongside my luggage; our combined weight will be used to calculate not only who and what is positioned where on the aircraft, but whether I'm allowed to fly at all. I scrutinize myself in the mirror to try to guess how heavy I am, then optimistically add a few more raisins to the pile.

There is no means of buying food on Bleaker Island. This is a fact both obvious—it's an island, unpopulated except for the farm manager and the owners, who spend only some of their

time there—and confounding. Everything I will eat while I
am there must come with me when I leave tomorrow. If I had
been better informed, I would have known that I could arrange
for provisions to be shipped out to me during my stay, but by
the time I learn this it's too late: the shipping plans are made
months in advance. Most visitors to the smaller islands like
Bleaker come either in the warm months as part of fully catered
organized tours, or are scientists on research trips with the
knowledge and expertise of academic colleagues and institu-
tions behind them. Not many—not any?—are writers who
looked at a map of the world and thought, whimsically, *how
about going here?*

I am worried about the food situation. Although I know I
have enough to stay alive, it's far from ideal, and I'm concerned
that hunger will affect my ability to work properly. In Stanley,
I'm too embarrassed to admit to my predicament, and insist
whenever anyone asks that I have more than enough food to
get me through my Bleaker stint. Somewhere in my mind, too,
is the idea that this is supposed to be a challenge, that I wanted
to get as far from my comfort zone as I possibly could, and the
difficulty of feeding myself for the weeks ahead is part of the
point of the trip.

I am surrounded by little heaps of sachets of powdered soup,
instant porridge, granola bars, and boxes of Ferrero Rocher
chocolates, which are a convenient combination of indulgent,
lightweight, and calorific. I calculate the total calories of everything I can afford to bring, and then divide it by the number
of days—forty-one– that I will spend on the island. It works
out that I will eat 1,085 calories per day. This, I tell myself, is
definitely enough to survive.

Maura pokes her head round the door. "They've announced

the times for tomorrow's flights on the radio," she says. "You're leaving at nine." She notices, then, the pile of food on the floor. She looks horrified. "That's not everything you're taking with you, is it?"

"Oh, no," I say, smiling, attempting nonchalance. "No—the rest is already packed."

"The Personal Assistant"

So that's a lesson about humanity for you," said David, looking up from his food. "For every visionary who builds a skyscraper, there are ten suicidal wankers waiting to jump off it." He gestured at Emily with his chopsticks as though she should be taking notes.

Emily stared at what remained of the steamed garoupa in front of him. It had been served whole, and he had prodded meat away from the spine in chunks. The plate was a mess of skin and scales and discarded flesh; only the head of the fish remained intact. Its mouth gaped, as though it were aghast at what had happened.

"Just make sure you don't call the suicides 'wankers' in the report," she said.

"Ha!" said David, more loudly than the joke deserved. He jabbed his chopsticks into the air again. A flake of fish flew off and landed on the cuff of Emily's blouse. She flicked it onto the tabletop, but it left behind a spreading stain on her sleeve.

"I'll have you go through and edit it out," he said. "But between you and me, Emily Blaine, wankers they are."

"Do you want to go over the schedule for tomorrow, or can it wait until the morning?"

"Morning." He leaned across and poured more wine into her glass. As she sipped at it, he sought out her eyes and held her gaze. "Everything OK, Em?"

"Fine." Emily looked away at the restaurant, where waiters were hovering beside tanks of live fish.

"I'm glad you're here," David said. "The brains of the operation."

"Damn straight," she said. "You're just window dressing."

He blew her a kiss across the table.

When they had finished eating, David signed the bill and gave Emily the receipt to charge to expenses. They wandered out onto Gloucester Road.

David asked, "Are you coming back to the hotel?"

"Yes," she said. "Where else would I be going?"

"I thought you might have plans."

She patted the binder that was jutting out of her handbag. It contained agendas for his meetings the following day; the numbers of drivers and the venues of the appointments; the names of VIPs and bullet-pointed information about each of them so that David wouldn't embarrass himself during introductions.

"The only plans I have are yours, David."

He put his hand on the small of her back and threw an arm out to hail a cab.

"That's why I love you," he said.

She laughed, then worried she had over-reacted. She knew that she was half a glass of wine away from saying, "I love you, too," though it wasn't true. It wasn't true, but she would have said it anyway.

. . .

It was the penultimate evening of their four-day trip to Hong Kong. David was the director of a research initiative investigating the socioeconomic, geographical and psychosocial determinants of suicide for what was called the "philanthropic arm" of an international bank; there was going to be a report, and a chapter on high-density, high-rise Asian cities. *Socioeconomic, geographical and psychosocial determinants of suicide.* Emily typed the words at least ten times each day; sometimes as she tried to fall asleep they would swim around her head. When she blinked, she saw them. Two months ago, when she had first started her job as David's assistant, they had seemed foreign and intimidating. Now, they rolled off her tongue as easily as her name, or David's.

In the taxi on the way back to the hotel, it seemed to Emily that Hong Kong was made up entirely of light: the headlights and tail lights of traffic, adverts sliding up and down the sides of buildings, the bright shop windows making everything in them look gold-plated. The hotel lobby: chandeliers dripping from the ceiling reflected everywhere in mirrors; the lift: illuminated numbers flashing and vanishing as she and David ascended, standing, she thought, a fraction closer to each other than other people might have stood.

She felt pressure building in her ears as they neared David's floor. Without saying a word, he reached out and tugged at the sash that tied the waist of her blouse. It came undone and sank to her feet. Emily stared forward as cool air seeped under her newly loosened shirt. When the lift opened at the thirty-fifth floor, she waited, not moving, as David stepped out. The doors slid shut behind him. She crouched to grab the sash and tucked it into her bag. She pressed two fingers against her neck as though she were sick and felt her heart, reliable, implacable, beating.

The phone was ringing in her room as she entered it. She kicked off her shoes into the dark in front of her and then tripped over them as she moved to answer the call.

"David?"

"Em, can you do me a favour?"

"Yes, of course."

"Are you in bed?"

She wondered whether he wanted her to say yes.

"I literally just got in the door."

She hadn't had time to turn the lights on. The room was illuminated by the city outside her window.

"I want to go to dinner tomorrow night."

"OK."

"So, can you book a table somewhere?"

"Of course." There was a silence. "This couldn't wait until the morning?"

She wondered then what David was doing. He was thirty feet beneath her, in a room more or less identical to hers. She walked towards the window. Behind her the phone cord stretched out like a leash. She pulled back the gauze curtain and looked out.

"I just thought I might as well tell you now."

"OK."

"Aren't you going to ask where, and when, and that sort of thing?"

"Yes," she said. She let her head fall forward so that her forehead pressed against the glass. Two parallel streaks of condensation plumed out beneath her nose. "What time?"

"Eight."

"Did you have anywhere specific in mind?"

"Yes. There's a place at the top of the ICC in Kowloon.

Highest building in the city; highest restaurant in the world."
He sounded as though he had rehearsed the line, or was reading
it from a page in a guidebook. "That's what I have in mind."

In a tower block across the street, two people were having sex. They were framed in their window. Emily peeled her
forehead back from the glass and wiped the smudge of her own
breath away. The couple were in a room about parallel with
David's. The woman was perched on the windowsill, her legs
splayed apart; she was holding her own ankles. The skin of her
back was white where it was stuck against the windowpane.
The man's hips jerked backwards and forwards against her. She
barely moved. She was looking away from him, to the side, at
one of her own feet.

"Table for two," David said.

Emily wondered whether he was standing at his window,
seeing the same thing. She wondered whether he had seen the
couple, and then decided to call her.

"I'll book it," she said. "I'll book a car."

"That's why I love you," David said.

"Anything else?"

There was another pause. He sighed and the receiver crackled.
"Nope."

"Goodnight."

"Goodnight, Em."

She waited for him to hang up and then let the hand holding
the phone fall to her side. She watched the couple across the
street: the man's awkward lurching and the woman's squashed
back. Below in the road, moving dots were people walking
about. In one of the blocks to her left, a boy was sitting on a
little balcony, his legs hanging through the railings beneath
him, his hair blown about by the wind. She felt dizzy. The hotel

was swaying again, as though it were contemplating throwing her and everyone else out. They would plummet like David's suicidal wankers, face first towards the pavement.

Nobody had seemed to know what to do with her when she arrived on her first day as David's new assistant. She stood in the lobby, too nervous to sit down, while the receptionist phoned someone.

"Emily Blaine is here. The new Carla. Who's supposed to be sorting her out?"

Emily walked along a line of photographs of people in the organization. They were black-and-white pictures; the heads floated on the wall in silver frames. She moved along the row until she came to David's portrait, which showed him standing at a podium in front of a large bar chart. He was grinning and biting a pen, one hand raised to make a point. The label on the frame read, "David Eliot, Director, Global Suicide Research Strand." She heard a click behind her and turned to see that David himself was there, cracking his knuckles and baring his teeth in a grin.

They had met before, once, at her interview, and she had been surprised then that he looked so young. Afterwards she had googled him and found the dates of his graduation from Cambridge; from those she had calculated that he was only two years older than her. Their lives, juxtaposed, made her feel miserable: he was directing his own research project for an international philanthropic organization; she was applying for any job that didn't require a first-class degree, or a master's, or two years of relevant experience. He was earning a six-figure salary; she had spent the three years since graduating from Birmingham University on an agricultural collective in Devon. She

had decided that she disliked him, and she disliked the organization. For a charity, it was too slick, too corporate, too full
of glossy photographs. Shouldn't they have spent that money
curing cancer and feeding hungry children?

After her interview, she and her flatmate had made a
drunken list of all the ways she could earn money that didn't
involve being David Eliot's assistant. "Run a coffee stand outside a Tube station," they had written. "Sous-chef. Bus driver.
Politician. Prostitute."

And then he had called her in person the next morning:
"Emily, do us the honour of joining the team," and she had said
yes, of course, thrilled, yes.

"Emily Blaine," said David.

"Hi," she said, "hi."

He shook her hand so tightly her knuckles ground together.
It took a fraction longer than she expected for him to release
the grip.

"Emily Blaine," he said again.

She had the impression, for a second, that he had fallen in
love with her. He was searching her eyes as though he and she
were very old friends, and had just been reunited.

"That's me," she said. She realized she had folded her lips
inwards in an awkward smile, and tried to correct it.

He continued to scrutinize her; she wondered whether she
had something on her face. She rubbed under her eyes, then
pulled her sleeves down over her hands. His gaze flicked to her
chest and then up again. She did the same, to check that all the
buttons of her blouse were done up.

"All right," David said, eventually, as though it had been she
who was holding them up. "Let's get to it. You'll have Carla's old
desk."

Carla's desk, when they reached it, looked to Emily as though Carla had not intended to leave for good. There was a notepad open on a page half-filled with notes and doodles of houses. She sat down and tried to imagine that it would soon look routine to her: the phone, the computer monitor, the tray of stationery, the view of Bloomsbury outside the window. She could make out the bulging green roof of the British Museum.

"Where's Carla now?" she asked.

She couldn't tell whether or not David's expression showed irritation.

"She moved to Hong Kong," he said.

When she opened the drawers, she found an open box of granola bars; a single red woollen glove; a packet of pills to relieve the burning, pain and urgency of urinary tract infections; and a card that said "Bon Voyage!" The card was filled with messages from people in the office. Emily read it on her lap as she pretended to study a health-and-safety leaflet. "It won't be the same without you," someone had written. "Our loss is Hong Kong's gain!" She checked every single name that was signed on the card; David's was not there.

Being David's assistant required the repetition of a few simple tasks. She booked flights, hotels, meetings, meeting rooms and dinners. She had a company BlackBerry and a company laptop. She was given access to his email account and was to handle all his messages except those that automatically filtered into a folder called "Personal etc." She should respond to routine or low-priority messages herself, and sign off as David. Anything that was high-priority she should mark with a red flag and find out in their daily meeting what response he wanted her to make.

"You'll get the hang of it," he said. "Basically, 'Can you speak to my university group' and 'Can you meet on Tuesday' equals

low-priority. 'What has happened to that £500,000 that's unac-
counted for in the budget?,' 'Should we cancel this project?,'
'Should we fire Emily Blaine?' equals high-priority."

"Got it."

"I'm joking. About the firing thing."

"Right."

"You're allowed to smile, you know."

"Sure."

He gave her his signature and told her to practise forging it so
that she didn't have to bother him with paperwork that needed
his sign-off. He had a meeting, he said, but it wouldn't take long.
She spent half an hour signing his name over and over again
on the bottom of the page of Carla's doodles. "David Eliot.
David Eliot. David Eliot." She wrote it so many times that her
brain switched off, and when she came back to herself, unsure
whether seconds or minutes had passed, she had begun to write
her own name instead. "David Eliot David Eliot Emily Blaine
David Emily Eliot Carla Carla." She tore the page off the pad,
folded it in half and slid it into the drawer with Carla's UTI pills.

She found a folder on her computer called "Carla admin"; it
contained details of Carla's contract. Carla, she discovered, had
earned several thousand more than she did. She raced through
the dry, legal language of the terms of employment, heart thudding, as though she were reading a thriller; she felt that she was
looking for something without knowing what it was.

A hand fell on her shoulder and her finger clicked to close
the window instantly. David was there.

"Everything A-OK, Emily Blaine?" he said. He half-smiled in
a way that made her think that he could tell what she had been
doing. He was standing very close, stroking her jacket, which
was draped over the back of her chair.

She wondered if she had turned pink. She felt sweat prickle

on the nape of her neck, under her blouse. She closed a couple more open windows on the screen: a spreadsheet and an email, to make it look as though she had been in the general process of shutting things down.

"Fine," she said.

He fiddled with the collar of the jacket, and found the price tag still attached. He tugged at it.

"What's this still doing on?"

She knew she was blushing; she could feel the skin of her face heating up.

"Thinking of taking it back?" said David. "Are you considering running away from us back to the farm?"

"No," she said. "No, I just forgot about it."

He reached over her and took a pair of scissors out of the box of stationery on her desk. She didn't turn but heard the sound of the snip behind her. The label hissed against the floor as it landed.

When she got home her flatmate was just leaving the house.

"How was it?"

"Boring," said Emily. "Nothing special."

"The guy's still a dick?"

"Yeah," she said. "Bit of a dick."

She sat on the back step and smoked three cigarettes in a row. She looked out at the grass verge that circled Stoke Newington's East Reservoir. She felt contorted and tired; for some reason her limbs ached. She blew smoke out in front of her. Then she went in, opened her new work laptop, and read every single email in David's "Personal etc." folder.

It was three a.m. when she finished, and by then she felt that she had become an expert, a leading authority on David Eliot. She knew about his relationship with his mother, and the affair his sister's husband was having and how his brother felt about keeping it secret from her. She knew his friend George was getting married and having a stag do that might be in Amsterdam but might be in Vegas. She knew that David signed emails to his family "Davey xx" and to his friends, "Dave," that he worried about his father cutting him out of his will, that he bought wildlife documentaries and books of first-hand accounts of combat in Iraq from Amazon, and bid on vintage computer games on eBay. And she knew that at 2:17 a.m. on the previous day, he had received a message entitled "Delete this!" from Carla L. Blakey. It contained a single line: "Stop it. Just stop it. Don't respond to this."

She dressed carefully, gazing at herself in the mirror of her hotel room. She had looked at online photographs of the restaurant David had chosen. It was all light and surface and reflection, like a half-hearted vision of the future.

She hadn't realized, when she had packed for the Hong Kong trip, that it would involve evenings out. She had only brought her work clothes: grey dresses and skirts that made her look, she thought, like someone pretending to be the sort of person who went on business trips to Hong Kong, and ate dinner in the highest restaurant in the world. She knew, staring at the image she presented in the mirror, that David would see through it. She had begun to feel that he could tell with a glance across a table or a desk or the seat of a taxi, what was inside her. He could tell that she had dreams about him; that she thought about him when she masturbated; that she had started deliberately matching her bra to her underwear, even though she didn't look good naked, even though she had several tattoos from her teenage years that she regretted, even though she knew that he would never see any of it anyway, not ever, and that she didn't understand why she wanted him to. He could tell, that she had been reduced by him to someone she would once have pitied.

She wore the loosest fitting of the grey dresses. She tied the waist with the sash she found crumpled in her bag.

In the hotel lobby, waiting for him, she paced between groups of people sitting in low, swivelling chairs. She kept catching sight of herself in the mirrored surfaces of the walls and ceiling and desks. When she sat down, her dress ran up her thigh; she thought about fixing it but decided, in the end, to leave it as it was. She was being stupid. It would be a night similar to the one before. It would not end with her and David in the same room, in the same bed, or balanced on a windowsill, naked and exposed.

"Em?"

He was standing in front of her, wearing a dark jacket.

"Did you get a haircut?" she asked.

He ran a hand over his head. "No."

"You look different."

He shrugged, but his face was tense. He was holding his phone in one hand, and fiddling with it.

"Car here?"

She nodded. He looked flushed, as though he had run there.

"Listen, Em, something's come up. I offered to take one of the professors from the university to dinner."

"I'm sure they can change the reservation," she said, "to three people. Do I need to arrange transport for him? Or her?"

David glanced at her exposed thigh, and Emily's hand twitched to cover it.

"Actually, Em, I think it might be better for me to handle this one alone. Saves you the trouble of calling them again, anyway."

She tried to keep her breathing steady, and her face expressionless. She knew that if she spoke at once her voice might tremble, so she looked away, as though something dull and irrelevant had just occurred to her. In the corner of her eye she could see David's feet shifting on the marble floor as he transferred weight from one to the other.

When she turned to him, she smiled. "I can use the extra time to sort out your schedule for next week."

David didn't miss a beat. "That's why I love you." His face relaxed a fraction. She thought perhaps he looked grateful.

When he was gone, she sat very still in the chair.

A man in a grey suit approached her with an extended hand saying, "Ms. Francis?"

She stared at him blankly before remembering to speak. "No, sorry." She felt as though he had woken her up.

The man backed off as though she had snarled at him. She watched him cross the floor and greet someone else. The woman smiled and shook his hand and he sat down beside her. By the lifts, a couple were kissing. Everywhere, there were people who had come to meet each other.

Emily slid her laptop out of her bag and logged onto David's email.

She had made daily resolutions not to check the "Personal etc." folder. It had become a sort of addiction, and she would begin each morning with a resolve that wore off, like her make-up, as time passed. By five o'clock she would be reading a string of emails planning George's stag party and an update from David's mother listing the possible dates she might visit his new flat, while rubbing at the smudged mascara over and beneath her eyes. She watched David's life like a soap opera. She would open the messages, highlight and copy them into a

Word document, then mark them as unread again in David's inbox. The process took about four seconds per message, and still she would sweat as she did it, and jump at small noises nearby; it seemed to her inevitable that she would get caught out at some point, and yet it was impossible to stop.

She opened the folder. There were a couple of new messages from Amazon, and one from a friend who was travelling in Uganda. And then she saw it, between a Facebook alert and a request for seller feedback from eBay: an email from Carla L. Blakey. "Re; Re; Re; Re: Delete this!" was the subject line. The message body read, "OK. But just for dinner. I mean it. Just dinner. You're going to try and make me drink but I'm not going to."

Outside the hotel, a doorman ushered her into a taxi. The car moved off and joined the oozing traffic on the roads. She could see, for most of the journey, the top of the ICC towering over the buildings on the other side of the water. It was typical, she thought, that David had chosen to meet that girl in a building she couldn't ignore. She would see it everywhere; it would remind her over and over again of him and Carla.

She wondered if he were already there. She wondered if Carla would be waiting for him, wearing a dress that was appropriate for the venue, and underwear that matched. When the car slowed behind a line of vehicles in the tunnel to Kowloon, she gripped the door handle so tightly her knuckles bulged, to prevent herself from punching the back of the driver's seat. They would be sitting opposite each other in the highest restaurant in the world; David would pour her a glass of wine that she would refuse to touch; he would lean forwards and she would be able to smell him. She would let her hand fall on the table, almost in the centre of it, and David would stare at her fingers, and make sure she knew that he was staring, before lifting them to his lips. The car edged forwards.

The hostess at the restaurant didn't want to let Emily through.

"Reservation?"

"My boss is here," Emily said. "I just need to give him something. It's important. It will take two minutes."

When she finally got inside, she felt exposed, and let her hair fall over her face as though it might disguise her. She had no good reason for being there. David would be appalled. The surfaces, the floor, walls, and ceiling, were clean and shimmering; her reflected face followed her from several angles.

She sat at the bar. She thought about turning around, going back to the hotel, ordering room service and getting drunk by herself. It would be the right thing to do; the mature thing to do. When they got back to London, she would start looking for another job, something more suited to her. She would dig out that stupid list she had made and work through each of the options, if necessary, right down to "Politician" and "Prostitute," because anything, anything would be better than this.

And then she saw David, sitting by the gaping glass window, and with him, Carla. David was facing the bar, but hadn't seen her. Carla, opposite him, had her back to Emily, so all that was visible was the curve of her spine under a sleeveless shirt, her cropped brown hair, an arm draped, perhaps a little awkwardly, over the corner of the table. Between them were the drinks, David's glass half-empty, Carla's untouched.

A waiter brought Emily a menu. She ordered without paying attention, something with whisky and vermouth in it. It felt as though she were watching David in a play, the way he was sitting and the way his face was making expressions she had never seen before: timid flickers between his eyebrows; nervous bites on his lower lip. His forehead and temples were glazed with sweat. There were blotches of red on his neck, blossoming out from under the collar of his shirt.

Emily drank four of the whisky cocktails and the room began to twirl and sway. When she stared hard, she could still focus on David. He had taken one of his shoes off, and had his foot on Carla's chair, between her legs. She had parted them slightly. She was sipping from her drink. Moments later, it was Carla and not David who leaned across the table. They kissed. David lifted a hand to hold the back of her head, and Emily, squinting through her blurred vision, saw that it was shaking like an alcoholic's.

When they pulled apart, Carla looked back over her shoulder. For the first time, Emily had a view of her face, and saw that she was old, in her early fifties at least but possibly nearer sixty. The skin around her eyes was loose and tired; her cheeks had begun to sag beneath her jaw. When she waved a hand to get the attention of a waiter, light flashed from the gold band on her ring finger and the flesh underneath her upper arm swayed.

David looked up and straight into Emily's eyes. He looked shell-shocked, as though someone had slapped him. Emily didn't move. He put a hand on the table and seemed to be about to rise and go over to her, but Carla reached out and trailed her fingers over his knuckles. He glanced again at Emily, and she tried to imagine all the things he must be thinking, and how much he must hate her. His eyes returned to Carla, who was talking, quickly, and her head was jerking as she spoke. When David replied, Emily thought perhaps he was speaking deliberately clearly, so she could read his lips.

"I love you," he said. "I love you so much."

Emily left the restaurant without paying. As the lift plummeted to the ground floor, she imagined she was falling. Outside the building, there was a fish market, with live crabs struggling against each other in shallow trays. The smell of salt and flesh filled her nose as she wandered through it. An elderly man was bent over a low table, decapitating eels. His knife fell rhythmically, like a heartbeat—chop, chop, chop—and the bodies continued to wriggle as they slid, headless, into a bucket by his knees.

A little way down the street, beyond the market and a line of parked cars, somebody screamed. Emily looked up and saw that something was falling; a body was falling from the sky. She began to run towards where it would land. She had the feeling that if she reached it in time, she might be able to catch it, like a bouquet tossed at a wedding. She tripped over a mat covered in shellfish and they scattered into the road as though they were trying to escape.

There was a sound, then, unlike any she had ever heard: a thud and a splash that was unmistakably the noise a human body made when it hit solid ground from a height. She felt certain, she somehow knew, that it was David, and when she had pushed through the shocked, silent crowd it took a moment for her to realize that it wasn't. It was a girl, young, not anyone Emily knew. She had landed, it seemed, feet first. Her bones had pushed through her shoulders. The legs and torso were mangled and bloody, but her head was whole and almost clean. The exposed skeleton was bright white against the red. Emily couldn't look away.

People began to call for help, and she joined them, screaming, "Help, help, help."

Spinning a Yarn

Bleaker Island is eight square miles of rock and mud off the south-east coast of an area of the Falklands called Lafonia. The land is owned by a farming couple called George and Alison, who divide their time between Bleaker and Stanley. Sometimes, then, the population of the island will be three, including myself, and sometimes it will be one, including myself. There are also sea lions, a thousand sheep, a small herd of cows, and a colony of gentoo penguins. There is no road. There are no trees.

The settlement in which I live is built on the narrowest strip of the island. This consists of George and Alison's house, large, positioned on the crest of a small incline, looking down on the other buildings, and a cottage that belongs to the farm manager and his wife, who are both away in England for the duration of my stay. There are two guest houses, which in the summer months will be full of groups on organized wildlife tours of the Falklands, but while I am here both are empty. I stay in the larger, more modern of the two: it has several bedrooms with the same geometric-patterned bed linen and curtains, a kitchen, a living room and the large sunroom, which is where I will write. Also in the settlement: a shearing shed, two other huts that serve unspecified agricultural purposes, and a wind turbine. This is the extent of civilization on the island.

For hours, I sit in the sunroom, staring at the view from the house: bald hillocks and the pattern of cloud-shadows sliding over them. When the wind drops, there are brief moments of unsettling quiet. Then a storm sets in, pelting hail and rain and snow against the glass roof, and I have the feeling that I am sitting inside the weather itself.

At night, it feels too dark to sleep. There's no phone service. The Internet connection comes and goes, sluggish and unreliable. I play music that doesn't fill the silence so much as sits on top of it.

I am regimented: I wake early and work my way through Canadian Air Force exercises—sit-ups, push-ups, ridiculous on-the-spot running—from a tattered old pamphlet I found in my parents' house before I left. I have the idea that the exercises will inspire in me a discipline that will last for the rest of the day, that a kind of military determination might enter me through the dusty pages of the pamphlet.

From my writing station in the sunroom—carefully disarranged laptop and notebooks, blue pen, black pen, pencil, *Bleak House*—with a view of the bay and the red-roofed shearing shed beyond it, I drink my whole day's ration of black instant coffee and make calculations. If a first novel should be 90,000 words (I read this somewhere on the Internet once, and cling to it as absolute, indisputable fact), then after my false starts and archive-digging days in Stanley, which produced only 10,000, I have 80,000 words to go. I am on the island for forty-one days, and will need to leave some time at the end for revisions—a week or so should be enough for that, surely?—so say that leaves me with thirty-two writing days: 80,000 Ð 32 = 2,500. I will write 2,500 words each day, and by the time I leave Bleaker, I will have drafted and revised a whole novel.

The figures scribbled down in the notebook are dry, unemotional. They look remarkably similar to the calorie calculations I made on the previous page: the total number of almonds and raisins in the extra-large bags brought from London, divided by the number of days on Bleaker. I am conducting a simple transaction. Over the course of my stay, I will consume a total of 44,485 calories, and convert them into one 90,000-word novel. I will be a Book Machine.

The less comforting realization following this exercise is that the number of words I am planning to write daily is more than double the number of calories I have budgeted to eat. The conversion that on one level seems so reassuring also appears unsustainable. Is it possible for a Book Machine to operate quite this efficiently? Will I run out of fuel? Will I come to a grinding, spluttering halt out here, alone, in the middle of the South Atlantic, with no hope of repair or rescue?

Mid-morning, I hear the sound of an engine thrumming alongside the whirr of the wind. Moments later the car appears in front of the house. George is behind the wheel, red-faced, hearty, and like everything else on the island, somewhat windswept. Even though I have only met him once, the day before, when he collected me from the airstrip and drove me to the house, the sight of a familiar face makes me feel jubilant with relief. He waves.

The passenger door opens and Alison, who is trim and impeccably put together, emerges. She wears make-up. She accessorizes. Her glamour strikes a dissonant note against the backdrop of the storm as she trots up the front steps and stamps crusts of mud from her boots. Her accent is distinctly plummy, with no trace of the Falklands' Somerset–Ireland–Australia twang when she pokes her head into the sunroom and says, "Hello there!"

"Hi," I say.

"Got a spare minute?" she asks.

I look down at the notebook in my lap, the scribbled numbers, the days stretching ahead and the task that is supposed to fill them. "Yes," I say. "Definitely."

"Great." Alison gestures with her head to the jeep behind her. "Come on then."

The wind hits me like a punch when I step outside.

Alison holds open the car door against the weather's buffeting and shouts, "Hop in! We're going to spin some yarn!"

Unsure if she means this figuratively or literally, I slide into the back seat of the car and the three of us bounce across the uneven ground around the bay towards the shearing shed. Inside, it is dark and echoey and smells of wood and petrol and animals. In one corner are the materials and apparatus for spinning: sacks of lumpy, yellow-grey wool, still pungent, and a wheel that looks like an instrument of torture. Staring at it, I feel a kind of stage fright. This is the sort of straightforward, practical task that seems mysterious and difficult to me, but obvious and easy to people like George and Alison.

I take the role with the least potential for disaster: positioned beside a sack, I pull knots from the wool, removing twigs and lumps of mud. I pass the de-clumped wool to George at the carder, a contraption that looks like two round-headed hairbrushes side by side. It churns out fluffy, clean fibres like candyfloss. Alison feeds these into the pedal-powered wheel and produces thin strands of wool, ready to be balled and knitted. We work in silence. The machine whirrs. Outside, the wind is howling.

After several hours of de-clumping, a layer of grease has built up on my palms. Soap and hot water don't shift it. Back in the house that afternoon my hands still smell of sheep.

To spin a yarn. To tell a story. You take something amorphous and lumpy and you order it. You twist it into something with a purpose.

It's encouraging to think of this as I sit down to commence my 2,500 daily words. It is easy to be a Book Machine, I tell myself. It is easy to be a spinning wheel. I am simply converting the things I have consumed—food, yes, but more importantly the stories I have read, dreams I've had, people I've met and conversations I've overheard—into a different form. My lanolin-coated fingers begin to type a sentence, then another.

It surprises me, that first day, to find the words coming so easily. It feels painless to put them down on the page. With nothing but the weather happening around me, Ollie and his adventures seem more vibrant and absorbing. From the sun-room, the grey view of the bay and muddy fields makes the story I am telling seem brighter in my mind. In less than two hours I check the word count and discover that I've already met my goal. I am a strange combination of exhausted and, perversely, a little disappointed. I have done military exercises, devised a master plan for my island time, spun wool with George and Alison and written 2,500 words, and it is only mid-afternoon.

My stomach rumbles suddenly and painfully. The rations I have set out for the rest of the day will at best take the edge off

the hunger, rather than satisfy it. In less than a week, George
and Alison will be leaving for Stanley and I will be truly and
utterly alone.

There is a lot of time ahead of me and perhaps not much to
fill it.

Bleaker is not large, but feels that way as I struggle against the
wind. I have been trying to get my bearings. The northernmost
and southernmost points are hard to reach by foot, so my early
explorations cover the middle section, where the landmarks
have reassuringly literal, solid names: Big Pond, Rocky Gulch,
Pebbly Bay. I learn the route between my house and the beach
where the aquamarine water looks, in rare glimmers of sunshine, discordantly tropical. As I cross the white sand, my foot-
prints are the only ones. It is like walking on fresh snow. Bright
sunlight followed by dark cloud-shadows. Wind. Bleached
pieces of bone underfoot.

At the far end of the beach, a penguin colony is forming.
The birds cluster together facing the ocean, from which others
emerge in threes and fours. When I get too close to them
they slide onto their stomachs, waggle their heads from side
to side and gargle distractedly; if I keep my distance, though,
they seem happy to ignore me, and continue to gaze out to sea
unfazed.

On these early expeditions, I reach places that, for the
remainder of my stay, I never find again: a dark, slimy cave half
hidden in the cliff face; a patch of coastline off which a huge
pillar of rock stands upright in the ocean, waves frothing at
its base. Later, I spend days searching for these spots with no
success. They begin to take on a mythic quality in my mind. I
plough through mud and hail, certain that if I cover enough
ground I will surely come across them again, but I never do.

Instead I find animals: a sea lion whose disturbed roar sends me scurrying backwards, stumbling over my own feet and mounds of tussac, heart pounding; fur seals sprawled like sunbathers on the rocks; giant wheeling birds above me.

Alison creates a phrase for my writing process. She calls it "doing my words." She pulls up outside the house each day around eleven and cheerfully calls over the roar of the wind, "Have you done your words today, Nell? Do you want to come for a drive?" I respond, "Yes, I've done my words," or "No, I haven't done my words yet."

You'd better stay in and do your words.

Get your words done so you can go for your walk before the storm hits.

Pop over for a biscuit when you've finished doing your words.

There are several days, early on, when the process does not go as smoothly as it did on my first attempt. Sometimes it takes me an hour, two hours, to settle on a single sentence. I am stuck on the outside of the story, blindly guessing what its real author would write. On those occasions it feels as though I am dragging the pages out of myself, letter by letter, and that each one is flat and dry and dead and weighty.

In these episodes of uncertainty, I cling to Alison's idea of "doing words" like a life raft, even after she and George have left the island, taking off in a little red plane that wobbles over the settlement before it disappears. "Doing words" is a much less daunting activity than writing. It feels matter-of-fact, as though each single word is a small, inevitable, finite, quotidian task. I do sit-ups and push-ups from the *Royal Canadian Air Force Exercise Plan*. I do my daily walk to the beach and back. I do my words.

. . .

A dream: You are in a place that looks like England. You are
with your friends. They say, *Come to a party with us!* And you say
you'll go. And then you look around and realize that you are in
fact 8,000 miles away from them, and completely by yourself.

Breakfast: a sachet of instant porridge made with water. A glass
of gelatinous fibre drink. Instant coffee (no milk). This is the
best meal of the day, and I eat it at the window, looking out
to sea.

Eleven o'clock: twenty-five raisins and ten almonds. I count
them out deliberately, obsessively, knowing that if I accidentally
take more, I risk hungry days later on.

Lunch: powdered soup, a granola bar, instant coffee.

Four o'clock: twenty-five raisins, ten almonds. Sometimes
in the afternoons I forage for extra supplies in the house: half a
bag of pasta at the back of a cupboard, a tin of peach slices, a jar
of chutney.

Dinner: powdered soup.

Just before bed: a single Ferrero Rocher, which I eat so
slowly that it lasts a full hour. I lick the chocolate shell as
though it were ice cream and nibble at the wafer beneath. It is
the pinnacle of luxury, a reward for making it through another
day. It is a nightly celebration that my return to civilization, to
warmth and conversations and company and a variety of views
from a variety of windows, is inching closer. In my notebook, I
muse on confectionery: "You never really want the hazelnut—
but imagine how it would taste *without* it and the whole *project*
of the Ferrero Rocher would fall flat. It would be bland and
empty. It simply has to have the nut."

The day that George and Alison left for the mainland, Alison came to the house and gave me a potato. "I had one spare," she said, as she held it out to me. In my hands, it was weighty, earthy, large—the opposite of powdered soups and fibre gel and painstakingly counted raisins. I took it to the kitchen and placed it, like a kind of trophy, on the counter.

It is still there. I am saving it for an emergency. It squats by the kettle, full of promise and reassurance, waiting to be called upon, and I spend a lot of time staring at it. I try to imagine the moment in the coming days or weeks when I will be so desolate and lonely that I will make the decision to eat it. What will have changed by then? Who will I be when I turn on the oven, pierce the brown skin, and bake the potato?

Bleaker House: COMPLICATION

nstalled in the Harbourside Hotel, where pastel-coloured bunting sagged from the lobby ceiling and a surly waitress served him instant coffee with UHT milk, Ollie tried to convince himself he was on holiday. From his room he had a view of the bay and the grey hillside beyond it. When, on the morning of his second day in the Falklands, sunlight briefly burst through the clouds, the water looked blue, almost as though it might be warm.

It was a week of his life, that was all. The flight back to England would be leaving the following Saturday, and in the meantime, all he needed to do was make a few enquiries about the identity of the letter-writer on Bleaker Island, pop over to see him or her, pop back, perhaps take a look at the museum he had passed on his search for accommodation, and then be on his way back to Oxford, and reality, and Mei. If he somehow managed to put a hundred pounds a month towards his credit-card bill, he could pay off the cost of this—What? Eccentric jaunt?—in just over eighteen months.

The lingering questions regarding who exactly he was popping to Bleaker Island to see, and how exactly one did pop to Bleaker, and what on earth he'd find once he did so, would be answered in due course, he was sure.

The proprietor of the Triumph Inn looked Ollie up and down with an expression somewhere between astonishment and disgust. It was dimly lit inside the pub, but Ollie could still make out the sheen on the man's forehead and the deep red hue of his sunburned skin. The man chewed his bottom lip and squinted, as though Ollie were a question on a quiz show. Behind him, shelves of sticky-looking bottles were decorated with faded streamers in red, blue and a colour that had once been white. A small notice was pinned to the wood; it showed a Union Jack, a silhouetted soldier and the words "Heroes Welcome in the Falkland Islands." Ollie had the distinct impression that the barman did not consider him a hero.

"Bleaker Island?" Ollie repeated.

"I heard you."

"Oh, good." Ollie tried a smile, which was ignored.

The barman didn't move, but continued to stare, blinking occasionally as though to ascertain whether or not he were dreaming. Eventually, he fixed his eyes on a point somewhere beyond Ollie's head, and said, "It's winter now. It's June."

"Yes," Ollie said, "I know. It's backwards here. I mean—not backwards, of course, just the opposite way round to, you know, England."

The barman held a glass up to the light, which revealed a pattern of smudges and encrusted dirt across its surface. He passed the sleeve of his shirt across it and moved to the pump, releasing a trickle of watery-looking beer.

"We don't get visitors in winter," he said.

"No, I suppose not."

"Not at this time of year we don't."

"No. Well, just me, I guess."

Ollie's investigations around Stanley had not yet yielded any useful information. The waitress at the Harbourside Hotel had given no appearance of understanding him when he had made his first tentative enquiry about the best way to get to Bleaker Island; neither had the woman at the West Store from whom he had attempted to buy a sausage roll; and now, at the Triumph Inn, it appeared he would have the same result.

The barman finished pulling the pint and slammed the glass down so that the beer sloshed against the sides and spilled. Ollie fumbled with his wallet, put money down, and turned to face the clusters of drinkers who had been watching him in silence since he had entered the pub. In the dim light it was hard to make out specifics. His gaze seemed to have a repellent quality, turning the onlookers away from him and back to their conversations. He had an impression of general, widespread sunburn and pairs of squinting eyes that didn't seem convinced they belonged together. Dartboards, gaping like open mouths, hung from the walls.

It was only when Ollie had downed his pint and resolved to leave that the barman grunted, "Ain't nobody on Bleaker Island no more. Not for years. Ain't nobody writing no letters from Bleaker Island."

"Oxford, you say?"

Nancy Fletcher, archivist, was standing in the doorway of

the Falkland Islands National Government Archives, surveying Ollie with an expression that suggested both scepticism and sympathy. Her eyes slid from his shoes, which were still mud-coated from his trek into town from the airport, to the ID card he was holding out to her. She yanked it from his hand and scrutinized it, raising it to the light as though she were checking for a fraudulent twenty-pound note.

"'Balliol College, Oxford,'" she read.

"Yes."

"I read a book about Oxford," she said, showing no signs of being prepared to move from her position guarding the entrance. "Stuffy place, the book said. A lot of murders."

She was in her mid-forties, smartly dressed in a way that didn't seem to fit with her surroundings: the lumpy white block in which the archives were housed; a grassy bank, slippery with goose droppings, that led up to the building from the road; and a view of a decaying shipwreck in the shallows that looked as though it were gradually melting into the water.

"It's that way," the waitress at the Harbourside Hotel had grudgingly told him, waving a limp hand down the road. "There's a sign. It says, 'Government Archives,' so you'll not miss it."

The "sign," when he eventually found it, was about the size of his palm, beside a doorbell labelled "Ring for Archivist."

"We get people here," Nancy said, frowning. "Journalists, who just want to dig around and turn up a stink."

"Right. I'm sure."

"It does nobody any good."

"I'm not a journalist."

"No Argentinian connections?"

He shook his head.

She was still holding his Oxford ID, turning it over in her hands. She glanced at the small print on the back, as though it might offer further insight into Ollie's motives.

"Normally the researchers write to me ahead of time. They ask me about the documents they want to see. They check what I have. They don't just turn up. It's appointment only. You can't just turn up, you know, out of the blue."

"Right, sorry," said Ollie. He was unsure whether to mention his family connections or not. He had resisted in his earlier enquiries, unclear what response it might provoke, and worried that friendliness might prove more awkward than the mistrustful hostility he had so far received. "Well, can I make an appointment?"

"I suppose so."

"Great. When can I come? When would suit you?"

Nancy considered him, tilting her head and staring at his face as though he were a watch. "Twenty minutes." She stepped back and closed the door sharply in his face.

Ollie stared at the barred entrance for a moment before turning and shuffling back down to the road. The shipwreck was straight ahead of him, and on the pavement, a small, damp bench, which seemed to have been placed to enable sustained perusal of the rotting carcass of the boat. Its helm had fallen away completely, and the remaining structure looked skeletal: an uncovered ribcage with nothing inside except birds and loose, waterlogged wood. The wind roaring in across the water was sharp and cold. Ollie began to shiver.

By the time the twenty-minute wait was over, he had lost feeling in his fingers. He fumbled with the "Ring for Archivist" bell again. Nancy appeared and showed him into a small cloakroom, where he reluctantly took off his jacket.

"No phones, no filming equipment, no pens," she said, when he emerged, still shivering, from the room.

He shook his head and held out his arms. "Nothing." When she continued to scrutinize him, he wondered whether he should turn out his pockets.

"All right," she said, eventually. She turned on her heel. "You can follow me into the Reading Room now."

The Reading Room turned out to be directly behind her, so it took only three steps for Ollie to follow her inside. It was small, almost entirely filled with a large, empty table. The walls were lined with shelves of documents labelled, variously, "1890s etc." and "A, B, C" followed by "U, V" and on the opposite side, "D, E." In one corner there was a desk that looked slightly bowed under the weight of an enormous, grey computer, which gave off a low, strained hum, as though it were over-heating.

Nancy sat down at the wide table, folding her arms. Ollie pulled out a chair and did the same.

"So, what is it you were looking for, Oliver?"

Ollie took a breath. "Well, as I said, my name is Oliver Graves. I've come to look for my father."

"And what would your father be doing in my archives?"

"My father's name is—was—Alsop Graves."

Once Nancy had recovered from her incredulity, and then from her excitement, her prevailing emotion appeared to be irritation.

"Alsop Graves had a son! He had a son! Why on earth didn't you say?"

"I—I don't know."

"Mad as a hatter, Alsop Graves. Mad as a box of frogs."

"Right," said Ollie. "Yes. Right."

She stood up and crossed the room to the computer, clicking the mouse several times and saying, "Wake up! Damn this machine. Wake up!" Eventually it whirred into life; the white screen lit up her face as she peered at it, typing rapidly.

"Is everything OK?" Ollie asked after a few moments.

She didn't look up at him, but continued to click and tap at the keyboard. Eventually, still without turning her gaze from the computer, she said, "What's your full name?"

"Oliver Graves."

"No, your full name. Middle name, too."

"Oh, er, Oliver Andrew Graves."

"Date of birth?"

"11th March 1983."

"Siblings?"

"Sorry?"

She glared at him. "Mother's maiden name?"

"I'm not sure I understand what—what this is for."

Nancy sighed and swung her legs out from under the desk. "I like to keep full records of the genealogy of all the families here, and I don't currently have an item for any surviving members of the Graves family. I'm trying to piece it together." She began tapping loudly at the keyboard. "This is a turn-up for the books. I'm not sure we've ever been completely missing a record like this before."

"Could you explain why it's so important to have everyone's family tree?"

When she had finished typing, she turned back to him. "Well, Oliver, in a community like this one—we're a close-knit bunch, and there's not many of us—it helps to know who is related to whom." She raised a suggestive eyebrow. "Sometimes when you see two young people getting together, you know, it's useful to have a quiet word, to point out certain things they already have in common."

"Right. It's just that I don't intend on 'getting together' with anyone."

"You're very like your father, you know," said Nancy, without looking up at Ollie. "I can see the resemblance now." She gave the keyboard a few more emphatic prods and then returned to the table, resuming her position opposite him, re-folding her arms. "So you've come to find out about your roots, have you?"

"Something like that. I was planning on going to Bleaker Island, actually."

Ollie waited for the response he had come to expect: a silence, and then the information that nobody lived there. Instead Nancy nodded and said, "Yes, of course, of course, to see the house, I suppose?"

"The house?"

"Your father's house. It's still standing, I should think, though I can't vouch for it myself. Nobody's lived there since your father's passing, Oliver, which was ever so long ago now— years and years."

"Nobody's lived there for twenty-five years? You're sure there's nobody there?"

"You could hire a plane to take you across," she said, "but you won't find a soul there, if that's what you were hoping for. It's not considered habitable, you know."

Things to Do on Bleaker Island

n the moments before a storm, you see a sheet of weather approaching the island over the water: a blurring of the line between the sea and the sky, the sound of the wind. Then it hits.

It snows for days on end. The ground is white: a blank page. The sea is a vat of spume and kelp, and on the beach, even the penguins look miserable, huddled together like the stranded guests of a black-tie dinner. A smothering cloud presses down overhead. The wind sweeps up settled snow as more falls. The island and the sky close in on each other.

When hail spits onto the roof of the sunroom, it makes the same sound as the waves dragging shingle on the beach.

From my writing station, I see only churning water and the foggy outline of a whale skeleton on the shore, its ribs unfolding like a line of parentheses. Downy geese huddle inside the vast skull, twisting their heads under their wings.

The storm has put a stop to everything. The radio in the kitchen reports that there are no flights between the islands. No cargo ships to bring supplies. Out at sea, invisible fishing crews vent their frustrations. Nothing is moving.

"Maybe it's happening," I tell my friend in Boston, also a novelist. "Maybe I'm getting depressed."

We are on Skype, taking advantage of the rare glimmer of an Internet connection. His pixelated face is unreadable. His jaw looks dislocated.

"What?" he says. "You're breaking up. You sound like a robot."

"Depressed," I say, slowly and loudly. "Depressed." And then the connection goes.

When I next get online, a few days later, there's an email from him.

Your situation reminds me of a story. It's about a very accomplished and dedicated artist, much like yourself, who one day decided to move to a remote island chain. There, he holed up for months, obsessively toiling on his next project. Of course, it was difficult. Of course, there were times when he wished he could go back. But the experiment worked. He returned from those distant islands with a masterpiece. He had transformed himself and his art. Back in the real world, he found he had surpassed all his peers. They tried to catch up to him. But none were willing to put themselves through what he put himself through. And so they couldn't catch him, and they still can't. Who was that artist? Kanye West. Of course, he took his retreat on the Hawaiian Islands, not the Falklands, but the same lessons apply. What I'm trying to say is, if he had never put himself through that experience, he would never have been able to give the world his *My Beautiful Dark Twisted Fantasy* (2010), his *Watch the Throne* (2011), and his *Yeezus* (2013).

What I'm really trying to say, Nell, is make your *Yeezus*. It's time.

He wants to make me laugh. He wants to cheer me up. But in this new snow-induced, self-pitying frame of mind, all I can think is that the premise of his joke—that Kanye's island experience and mine are so hilariously unalike—somewhat undermines the comfort it was supposed to bring.

I am doing the real work of being alone, now. Alison and George were wonderful and generous and kind while they were here, but their company during my first days on the island felt like cheating somehow. That wasn't how it was supposed to be. I came here to be by myself. Now that Alison and George are in Stanley, the thing I came so far to sample—solitude—is entirely mine.

There is a definite change in the way I feel now that I am truly by myself, but the change is not, in fact, that I am lonelier. Rather, I am suddenly, passionately hungry.

In the afternoons, I am too ravenous to read or write or think straight, so I walk to distract myself. I stomp out from the house along the shore, past the whale skeleton, the shearing shed and the settlement outhouses, up towards the cliffs and, further off, the beach and the penguins. I like facing out to sea and being pummelled by the wind. I even like the sharp bite of the cold on my fingers and toes, the experience of gradually losing sensation in my extremities. I like it because it distracts me from my unrelenting desire to eat.

At first, the hunger manifests itself in my stomach: outraged rumbling, cramps. Then, later, I stop feeling it anywhere except as a thick, boring headache that settles over the back of my head like a vice. I can't concentrate on words or thinking. All I can do is walk.

Hemingway claimed his impoverished hunger helped him appreciate art: In Paris "you could always go into the Luxembourg museum and all the paintings were heightened and clearer and more beautiful if you were belly-empty, hollow-hungry. I learned to understand Cézanne much better and to see truly how he made landscapes when I was hungry." But, Hemingway, I think, how can that be? How can it be that while you reached new, even greater levels of artistic comprehension, I am dizzy and grumpy and too stupid to read more than a few pages of *A Moveable Feast* on my Kindle at a time? As I stomp through mud and stones towards a herd of uninterested cows, I engage in furious debates with him in my mind—and gradually, though I don't realize it at the time, out loud.

Hunger is good discipline, Hemingway says. I grumble back, kicking through puddles, that earning enough money to feed yourself properly, or packing enough supplies, would actually show better discipline. *You God damn complainer,* says Hemingway. *You dirty phony saint and martyr. Hunger is healthy and the pictures do look better when you are hungry.*

I am, above all, irritated. With myself for not bringing more food. With the island for not better catering to my appetite. With my fuzzy, aching brain for not being more lucid. And with Hemingway for being so macho and determined about the whole thing.

I worry that my writing is bad because I am too hungry to think straight.

For a while, I give up counting the passing days. Instead

I track words amassing and food supplies dwindling: 35,000 words done and twenty-seven Ferrero Rochers left; 40,000 words, twenty-five Ferrero Rochers. When I do finally consult the calendar on my laptop to try to locate myself on the endless progression of dates, it is surprising that only a fortnight has passed since I arrived, that my absolute isolation has so far lasted a single week.

How to fathom the bleakness of Bleaker Island? First, consider: *Bleaker than what?* I had vaguely wondered this before arriving. Now, I know: it is just bleaker. I have begun to occupy a comparative world: I am colder, hungrier, more isolated. There is an unspoken final clause: *than ever before*.

But I sought it out; I looked at a map of the world and the place I chose to go was here.

And haven't I always done this, I wonder, as I pace from one end of the sunroom to the other, occasionally knocking into wicker chairs positioned for guests to admire a sunset that is happening behind the clouds and snow banks. Haven't I made a habit of leading myself to bleak places in the hope that it will be good for me? I stop pacing and look out at the water. The snowfall has made visible the tiny islands that surround Bleaker. Normally their grey-green rocks blend imperceptibly into the grey-green sea, but now they are bright white, dotting out towards the icy horizon.

Perhaps I have, consciously and less consciously, spent my entire adult life on a self-indulgent, agitated tour of bleakness.

There was Hong Kong; the Euro Hotel in Clapham where I lived after I left Will; and the estate in Deptford, its endless concrete corridors an archive of unsavoury realities: needles, used condoms, and once, a woman gutting fish outside her front door, entrails spilling out across her doormat and feet. There were night shifts at a shelter for asylum seekers in Coventry, where I handed out cups of lukewarm curry to shuffling, exhausted, traumatized people who could never meet my eye. Later, I worked in a refugee camp in the West Bank, where small boys paraded with weapons longer than their arms, and where my housemates and I asked, every time we heard a bang, "Gun or firework?" One summer, in Syria, I watched a small boy fall forwards from the seat of the tractor he was driving and under its wheels. That evening his brothers took buckets of soapy water to wash the dead child's blood from the road.

But it is now, here, on Bleaker Island, that I am most afraid of getting depressed.

"Why do you do it to yourself?" my mother wonders, sounding distant and somehow celestial over a bad Skype connection.

I repeat this question to the novelist friend. "That's the thing about being a writer," he says. "Every bad experience you have is good material."

My twenties appear to me, now, as a frantic and masochistic quest for good material, a wild attempt at atonement for an uneventful childhood.

At Boston University, I taught an undergraduate class on life writing. I nominated one of the students to give a presentation on two set texts: Orwell's *Down and Out in Paris and London* and Joan Didion's *The Year of Magical Thinking*. The student was very young, and very handsome, and had raised scars criss-crossing his forearms that he made no effort to hide. His female peers thought he was attractive. When I called him forward to present, he stood at the front of the room without notes, and gazed at his classmates for a long time. I thought he might be high. Then he said, "The key to interesting life writing is to lead an interesting life," and sat down.

Three months later he was dead, having, in the delicate words of his mother, "lost his battle with drugs and depression."

A dream: You and your friends are in a military-style line-up, being inspected by a meticulous and irritable hairdresser. You can hear him further down the line, barking instructions for the removal of split ends. Some he passes over with slight nods of approval. As he approaches, you feel your anxiety rise. He stops in front of you. He takes a lank lock of your hair between finger and thumb, and says, with disdain, "What is this?" You splutter. You try to explain. You realize with a creeping guilt that you haven't used conditioner in months, that you have been tying your hair behind you, out of your own sight, ignoring it as much as possible. "Flat! Lifeless! You've let all your layers grow out!" he roars. He is crimson with rage. Finally, your voice returns, "But I'm on an island!" you say. "I'm on an island!"

In my notebook I write, "Things to Do on Bleaker Island in July" and then leave the page blank. This strikes me as extremely witty.

Then I make another list called "Things to Do on Bleaker Island in August":

1. Bite your nails.
2. Watch the water for sixteen hours without interruption. It changes colour with each shift of cloud and rain and wind. Create names for the shades, like gradations of paint on a chart. Seal-flank grey. Black-dog grey. Gangrene grey.

3. Develop fears: of the wind turbine spinning off its post, decapitating you, leaving your headless corpse to be discovered by caracaras; of silence; of small noises; of the roar of the wind or the absence of the roar of the wind; of your own shadow. Or—

4. Build a relationship with your shadow. Try to learn its many forms in relation to the position of the obscured sun.

5. Become paranoid: somebody is poisoning your coffee. Wake up in the middle of the night with a headache, and then, in the morning, cower by the toilet bowl, throwing up water and bile. Retch. Tiptoe downstairs and observe the coffee jar from a distance. Closer, check the seal for signs of tampering, but find no evidence of foul play. Scurry up to vomit again.

6. Learn to distinguish between the creaks and taps and groans of the building in the wind, and the sounds of a person actually entering the house. It is never a person entering the house.

7. Make note of your disturbing dreams, and in the margins, wonder, "How on earth did I end up here? What happened to me, that this is now my life?"

Bleaker House: FURTHER COMPLICATION

Freezing air grated in Ollie's throat. It was dark. When he looked into the space in front of him, he saw a broad expanse of black, punctured by occasional glints on the water. There was a pale, uncertain moon at his back, casting weak light; enough to know he was on the shore, and beyond that, nothing. Wind slid off the ocean into his mouth and eyes. Gravel shivered as the waves ground over it. From further off, a strangled shriek made him look up into the blank space. The noise repeated, louder, then closer, until he could just make out the shape of an animal—he couldn't tell what; he thought it had both ears and wings—by his feet in the water. He scrabbled backwards until he reached the path that ran along the coast. The cry sounded again, further off, and then there was a splash, and then silence.

In the cold, he had lost feeling in his cheeks and fingers; his legs felt limp as he stumbled across the uneven ground. Beneath his feet: rocks, sand, thick clumps of long grass that tangled around his ankles, mud. He was hungry. He was tired. How long ago was it that the tiny red plane had deposited him on Bleaker Island, that the pilot had waved him off with a cheery grunt, the suggestion that Ollie's ancestral home was "just yonder near the cliffs," and a promise to return in a couple of days? Not more than two or three hours, surely. Long enough for night to fall. Long enough for Ollie to get more profoundly lost than he had ever been.

He turned away from the sea. Land rose before him towards an invisible summit. He began to climb in the hope that, higher up, he might get a glimpse of the house. He had packed supplies—food, a gas stove, a sleeping bag—but if he failed to find the house, it was all for nothing. Nancy had assured him it was still standing.

He kept his eyes fixed on the moon, but noticed with dread that a blanket of cloud had started to creep across its surface. He sped up as the light began to shrink, feeling suddenly that this was an escape route, a door that was closing before his eyes.

The moon vanished into an uninterrupted expanse of darkness. Ollie's boot caught on something and he fell. The rucksack on his back slid forwards and thudded against his head as his hands sank into thick mud. He lay, panting, too cold to feel pain, and began to consider the possibility that he was really going to die: of exposure, exhaustion, embarrassment. He hoped it would be soon.

He didn't move. Soon his breaths slowed and his mind settled into a rhythm: *Robinson Crusoe,* Chapter Four: "I am cast upon a horrible, desolate island, void of all hope of recovery." The sentence looped over and over in his head as the wind rushed around him. "I am cast upon a horrible, desolate island, void of all hope . . ." The repetition felt soothing, until the words began to twist and dart away from him, contorting: "I am horrible upon a cast-iron land"; "I am cast upon a hobbling despot"; "I am aghast in a wobbling, deathly asylum." He would pass out before he felt really bad, he told himself. At least, then, if he were going to die, he wouldn't have to be there to experience it. He wondered if his eyes were open or shut. When he tried to operate the lids they seemed separate from him, beyond his control. He guessed they were closed. "At last I am incorrigible, despite my silence, void of all globe-trot or blubbering."

In the far-off darkness, something stirred. It seemed to Ollie like a tiny insect, a firefly, darting across his field of vision. It began to grow, like the end of a tunnel; like an odd, extending arm. This was what it felt like to die, then. He lay still, fascinated. In his dying moments, he did not go toward the light. The light was coming to him.

The beam got closer still, expanding, tilting, illuminating gravel, rocks, clumps of weed and eventually Ollie's own hands submerged in mud. Then it stopped.

Over the wind and waves, the light began to speak. "Identify yourself," it hissed.

Ollie regained control of his eyes and blinked several times before he understood what he was seeing: the round face of a torch, the edges of fingers gripping it, inches from his nose. He pulled his hands until they came out of the mud, one by one, with wet, sucking noises. He pushed himself up, first to his knees, then his feet.

"A nobbly, desktop icon," he spluttered, through numb lips, in the direction of the torch and the invisible person behind.

"What language is that? Are you one of those Chinese off the fishing boats?" came the hissed reply.

"A horrible, desolate island!"

"State your purpose! State your name!"

A strong gust of wind nearly knocked Ollie off his feet. "Oliver," he said at last. "Oliver Graves. I've come about my father."

The beam of light slid shakily down from Ollie's face to the ground, and for the first time, Ollie got a sense of the person controlling it: a slight, sharp-edged female figure—a large child or small adult—and a faintly illuminated curtain of fair hair.

"Oliver Graves?" she said. "Really Oliver Graves?"

"Yes."

"Oliver Graves," repeated the girl. "I thought you'd never come."

Two, Not One

The room, which was strewn with papers and nearly filled
by a great writing-table covered with similar litter, was, I
must say, not only very untidy, but very dirty . . . But what
principally struck us was a jaded, and unhealthy-looking,
though by no means plain girl, at the writing-table, who sat
biting the feather of her pen, and staring at us. I suppose
nobody ever was in such a state of ink.

—ESTHER'S NARRATIVE, *BLEAK HOUSE*

eslie Epstein is a man who teaches writing with rules.
There are many, outlined in a document called "Tips
for Writing and Life," which he distributes annually to
each incoming cohort of MFA students, and which is referred
to thereafter as the "tip sheet." The phrase "tip sheet" makes
Leslie's rules sound friendly, as though they are mere suggestions.
They are not mere suggestions. They are specific. "Have

in mind between 68 and 73 percent of the ending before you begin. In narrative prose, as opposed to indented dialogue, write, on average, two-and-a-half paragraphs per page, never six or seven or ten. Avoid large abstract nouns, particularly those ending in 'ness.' Limit your similes to two a page. Do not write satire."

Leslie's students learn, over the course of their apprenticeship, that these rules are both tongue-in-cheek and very serious. You will be castigated for using the word "happiness," for disrespecting your own characters, for spelling "all right" as one word, for paragraphs that are too long, for ellipses . . .

You also learn that one of the things Leslie loves above all is a story that breaks his rules and still somehow "works." These are rare.

One of Leslie's tips, which I think about a lot on the island, is "Two, not one." By this he means that the interest of a story lies in the interaction between two characters. A narrative that stays in the interior thoughts of a single character alone is more likely to fall flat and lose the interest of the reader. You need two—you need at least two. A more familiar way of putting this, a staple tenet of the creative writing workshop, is the assertion that narrative, or drama, requires conflict.

I have put myself in a situation that is, on paper, one, not two. My conflicts are predominantly internal: with moods, and memories, and, worst of all, dreams. When I send Leslie an excerpt from my novel, in which Ollie arrives on the island at night, loses his way and contemplates his own death, the response that bounces back into my inbox almost at once confirms my anxieties on this point: "Well, Nell, when you go to an island with no one on it, it's not surprising that you write a Onesey instead of a—recommended—Twosey."

. . .

Apart from the *Royal Canadian Air Force Exercise Plan*, I only
have two books with me in paper form. The first is David
Shields's *Reality Hunger*, which I finished in one sitting on the
plane from Santiago and which lies at the bottom of my case for
the entirety of my Falklands stay. And the second is *Bleak House*.
Other things I read on a temperamental, scratched Kindle—
though I'm a slow reader in general, once I overcome the initial
fuzziness of hunger I manage to get through a book most days
here—so *Bleak House* is the only novel I have with me that I can
actually hold: it has covers, pages, mass. In this way it assumes a
presence that my other reading doesn't. I read it in bed, wearing all my clothes, usually right after lunch, and so it becomes
part of the fabric of my days, like the raisins and almonds and
the nightly Ferrero Rocher. I could have brought more food
with me; instead I brought this decadent, weighty book. I like
its heft. I like its expansiveness. I like the familiarity of the
London it describes. The novel names the city, and the city, as I
remember it from afar, recalls the novel over and over, in dark
streets, in rain, in contortions.

The picture on its cover—a looming building with dark
windows, black-and-white—makes me think of the bookshop
on Charing Cross Road where I bought it years earlier: drizzle
making the street outside look monochrome; the smell of
coffee drifting down from the cafe on the top floor. The page
margins are marked up with scrawls from lectures at university,
when I wrote things like "Weather! Atmosphere!" and "Psych.
of Realism" and "Feminine modesty / Unreliable narrator?" in
blurry-edged pencil.

Sometimes on the island, I dream about London, and in
those dreams it is a strange amalgamation of the way it was as I

last saw it—warm, familiar, 2013—and the way it appears in the novel—fog clogged, Victorian, full of scrap paper.

Life lived as a onesey doesn't always feel that way. My days are filled with interactions that seem, as time passes, increasingly real: my debates with Hemingway subside as my stomach shrinks and adjusts to the diet of powdered food, but others take their place.

My novelist friend, still on a mission to buoy me up, sends me excerpts from Dickens's letters: "How I work, how I walk, how I shut myself up, how I roll down hills and climb up cliffs; how the new story is everywhere—heaving in the sea, flying with the clouds, blowing in the wind; how I settle to nothing, and wonder (in the old way) at my own incomprehensibility." In my mind's eye, Dickens rolls and climbs all over Bleaker Island; the image is so vivid it is disconcerting. The hills and cliffs and sea and clouds and weather of the letter become my hills and cliffs and sea and clouds and weather. Dickens strides up the incline towards George and Alison's house, and sets out across the beach. He discovers parts of Bleaker that even I haven't found—caves and peaks and new animals—seeing and not seeing, busy with his work.

He seems to inhabit both himself and his landscape so easily; to fit so snugly into the mould labelled "Author." When I see him setting out on his adventures across the island, the hail doesn't sting him. When he approaches the penguin colony, they do not slither away from him on their stomachs but instead hold their ground, and allow him to join their solemn vigil. When he reaches the little hut by the airstrip, he doesn't stare forlornly at the "Welcome to Bleaker Island" sign and ponder how on earth he ended up here, whether the story that possesses him is the right one, whether it is even worth telling. Instead, he wonders (in the old way) at his incomprehensibility. He marvels at the creative forces he finds within himself.

By contrast, as I continue my own exploration of the island, rolling down hills and climbing up cliffs, I engage in a series of ongoing battles with frustratingly comprehensible things: the wind, primarily, which throws the toggles of my coat into my face with stinging frequency, with my own under-fuelled muscles that sometimes make a leisurely downhill stroll feel like a marathon through quicksand; and, lately, with a caracara that follows me on my walks with the persistence of a shadow.

I worry that these are the things that possess me. These are the things that are everywhere. And if that is the case then Ollie, my lone, onesey of a character, cannot be as real to me as Esther Summerson and John Jarndyce and Lady Dedlock and Miss Flite and Guppy and Jo and Richard and Ada and Inspector Bucket and all the countless others were to Dickens.

There are several caracaras on the island: large, black birds of prey, sharp and clever-looking. When they land, they plummet clumsily into the mud, then cock their heads to one side to examine you as though assessing whether or not you are a flight risk. They are attracted to things that shine, and anything red that resembles fresh meat. The feathers around their eyes give their faces a permanent scowl. And there is one bird that seems to have made it his business to hound me off Bleaker for good.

I am walking along the coast, south of the settlement. It is coming to the end of a bright, gold-lit day; for once there has been no rain. Beside me is the sea, dark blue. The sun is at my back and my shadow is leading the way in front of me, rippling over the stones and bones and moss. My silhouette is dark, its edges crisp, and when I glance at it I notice that inches above mine is another shadow: the perfect outline of a large bird, wings wide, talons dripping down towards my scalp. I look up and see the caracara, about six inches above my head. I shriek and duck and the bird changes course in the confusion, thudding down in front of me, stopping me short. He tilts his head to one side and scratches the ground with his feet. He looks as though he is about to charge.

When I was in Stanley, Maura told me that caracaras sometimes eat the eyes and tongues of lambs. This detail comes back to me now, and I raise my hands to my face. I peer through my fingers at the bird, which is hopping up and down, and then I break into a sprint for the settlement. My shadow and the bird's precede me on the ground, the space between them shrinking.

I dive for shelter in the first of the farm outhouses and slam the door shut behind me. Seconds later, I hear the crash and scrape of the bird's feet as it lands on the roof. Its talons scrape along the metal: scratch, scratch, scratch.

Each time I read a novel it leaves me with two stories at the end. There is the one the book deliberately tells, its plot, characters and setting, and then there is the story of my reading, the time, place and atmosphere around me as I turn the pages. *Wuthering Heights* transports me to the summer after I turned seventeen, when I missed a record-breaking heat wave because I was inside, lying on my bed with a brain full of wilderness and rain and fog. *Madame Bovary* takes my mind not only to Normandy but also to the dim, damp flat in Leamington Spa that I shared with seven other students in my second year of university, where I read to the soundtrack of the smoke alarm constantly squealing, and the voices of people all around me arguing, laughing, hooking up, breaking up.

. . .

Now, a strange and unreliable relationship forms in my mind between the worlds of *Bleak House* and Bleaker Island. This happens in the same way that I suppose horoscopes make sense to believers in astrology. A generality, framed in the language of intimate experience, strikes you as uncanny and insightful: "As the moon completes its sojourn in your sign, you'll be reaping the benefits of the energy you've put into your relationships over the past year. When an opportunity comes your way in the middle of the month, take hold of what you've earned." Like a true believer, then, and with nobody to correct my magical thinking, I start to see the novel as a meaningful guide to my experience in the Falklands and to my own work of writing: I make connections, see patterns. *Bleak House* is full of writers. It is full of lonely people. It is full of characters desperately hoping for things that may or may not come to them. And it is full of missing scraps of paper. It is about so many things that its main concern is the many-ness of the things about which it is concerned, circular and teeming and self-involved. In this sense, I am able to acknowledge a mismatch: in *Bleak House*, there is a surplus of stuff; on Bleaker Island, I have the bare necessities and a surfeit of emptiness. But still, among the many preoccupations of *Bleak House* is this central concern: the strange ways families fracture and lose each other; the equally strange ways they come together again.

I spend a lot of time thinking about Esther and Lady Dedlock: the mother and daughter separated, simultaneously oblivious and recognizable to each other. Ollie is Esther, on an unwitting journey to find his origins.

And then I think about Richard, ward of the interminable Jarndyce and Jarndyce court case, who becomes obsessed with his potential inheritance and descends into a state of manic, avaricious delusion. Ollie is Richard, willing his ancestors to make sense of his life for him, to tell him who he is and what to do and make everything easy.

Folded into the back of my copy of *Bleak House* is a printout of an article I found before I left, which details the plans Dickens made for the novel. His notes are haphazard and hard to follow: chapter headings and character names; the odd, scrappy line of dialogue; enigmatic directions for action.

> *Skimpole and Boythorn brought together? Next time*
> *Miss Flite's friends?—Her birds? Yes slightly. The birds. Not the*
>   *friends.*
> *Old Turveydrop—Pathetic too—blesses people—My son! etc.*
> *"I have forgotten to mention again—at least, I have not*
>   *mentioned—"*

The notes are cryptic. I think perhaps, if I can just decipher them, if I can crack the code, I'll know how it's done. I'll be able to tell stories the way Dickens tells stories. So I make complicated, frenzied charts, mapping the trajectory of *Bleak House* against that of my own novel: Ollie's search for his father, his voyage into the unknown, plotted alongside the failed collision course of Esther and Lady Dedlock.

When I look at these plans the next day, I find my own scribblings almost as indecipherable as Dickens's.

Trapped by the caracara, I wait in the dim hut. The bird is audible above me: fingernails down a blackboard, its talons across the ripples of the corrugated-iron roof. I watch my own breath and crouch in a corner, pulling my knees up inside my coat to try to preserve heat. I know this is ridiculous, that the bird will not attempt to eat my eyes, but still I can't coax myself out into the open.

It is dark by the time I work up the courage to open the door and sprint home.

In the fiction workshop at BU, Leslie liked to ask questions like, "What is the greatest novel in the English language?" and "Who has the biggest heart in twentieth-century letters?" and, of a story being workshopped in class, "What is the true ending to this work?" The person to offer the correct answer (*Middlemarch*; J. D. Salinger; that the protagonist goes back to the house and asks for a glass of water from the woman he loves) would be rewarded with a coffee candy, retrieved from Leslie's satchel and thrown roughly in the direction of the student's head. Around the end of our last semester, I read an interview with him in which he says, of his teaching practice, "I throw coffee candies around when they get the right answer. And there is no right answer, but I pretend there is in fiction writing."

A List of Everything I'm Ashamed Of

fall into the habit of obsessive self-monitoring. Like the weather, minute changes in my habits or thoughts seem suddenly worthy of careful study. I give up using an alarm clock, and instead keep meticulous notes of when I go to bed and when I get up. I hope this exercise might reveal something profound about myself, but at the end of it, all I have is a list of dates and times and a general sense that, when left to my own devices, and with literally nothing better to do, I fall asleep around half past ten and wake up just before seven. I do not know what to do with this information.

In the same spirit of self-scrutiny, I keep a note of the fluctuations of my mood, patrolling for sustained deterioration, but also with the idea that I might discover some convenient pattern: that I am always more cheerful before lunch, for example, or that I get a little sad around four o'clock. Perhaps my best ideas always come to me just before I go to sleep? I think of people who know these things about themselves—the ones who wake up to do two hours' work before breakfast because that's when they are most productive—and wish I were more like them. I do not know when I am most productive. Despite my charts, reports and hourly checks, no trends emerge.

One morning I wake to find that eight sheep have wandered into the settlement and are grazing in front of the house. I cannot take my eyes off them. I wonder if they are supposed to be here, or whether they've broken through a fence; I wonder whether I should do anything about them. They disturb the geese, who squawk and fuss. They blunder along the shore, scattering loose stones into the water. When I check the time, I realize I have been watching the sheep for nearly two hours, with more attention and intensity than I would pay any TV show at home.

In front of me, my laptop: a blank page. I cannot remember what I was writing. I do not know what I should write. When I scroll up through the document—the novel that has grown day by day—it is suddenly hard to read the words. It is as though it has been written by somebody else, in a language I do not know well.

I blink and gently slap my cheeks. I give myself a pep talk about concentration, about getting things done, about the end being in sight and how it will feel to leave Bleaker Island with a complete novel. I force myself to read earlier chapters, to get back into it, but the writing makes me wince. I fall to scrolling through the other bits of writing I have on my computer: stories, fragments of memoir, searching for something that will pull me back into my own voice.

· · ·

At ten past three on a Tuesday, after two weeks alone on the
island, it occurs to me to compose a list of everything I've ever
done that I'm ashamed of.

The thought drifts into my head and stays there, tantalizing
and horrifying. I am transfixed by the idea, struck that such
an account could exist and that by merely imagining it, I have
somehow already called it into being. For a long time, I sit
with my pen hovering over the page. I begin to write the title,
and then stumble on the grammar of the sentence. "A list of
everything I'm ashamed of." "A list of everything of which I am
ashamed." I have to choose between the dangling, inelegant,
incorrect "of," and the pompousness of grammatical precision.
And then it strikes me as ridiculous that a person who has lived
such a dastardly, reprehensible existence as I have is worrying
about syntax, rather than the trail of ruined lives and misery
I have left in my wake.

Memories of past transgressions hatch in my mind, and as I
stare through the window at Bleaker's bottomless bleakness,
I begin to feel appalled by myself. I have lived despicably. I have
told lies, hurt people, disregarded the feelings of friends and
lovers, disrespected my parents and behaved arrogantly towards
my teachers. I left Will when he needed me. I have used people
and exploited situations out of curiosity, or to have something
to write about. When I was five, my brother hid my teddy bear,
and in response I attacked him so violently that he still has
scars on his face, over twenty years later: two parallel white
lines beneath his left eye. There are countless other worse
things, of course. I am a monster.

My pen dips to the page, then rises again without making a
mark. If I write this list, there will be nobody to tear it up and
say it doesn't matter. I will be alone, on a remote island, with

a list of everything shameful I've ever done and nobody here to discredit it. Those good people—the ones I have treated so poorly my whole life, the friends and family who have supported and loved and listened to me—are not here now to offer yet more help.

If I write this list, it will exist even more solidly than it does now in my head, in its churning, amorphous, nightmare form.

I drop the biro, tear the page from my notebook, and fold it in half.

"Misadventure"

Billy Keys was shaving when he heard the crash. He froze, razor halfway between his chin and the sink. It sounded as though there had been an explosion behind him in his bedroom. He considered ignoring it, but after a couple more strokes with the blade found himself turning and walking in the direction of the noise.

He stopped in the doorway.

"Fuck."

The window of his bedroom was no longer there. In its place, black branches jutted through the frame, and rain was streaming in from outside. The stench of grease and batter drifted up from the chip shops on Camden High Street, along with the smell of petrol. The branches were bare. They belonged, Billy realized, to the dead tree that had been rotting on the street outside, swaying in high winds, threatening to fall. The council had posted a notice on the trunk announcing a date for its removal, but the date had passed and the tree had remained.

The branches pushed in like hands pointing at the damage they had done. The room did not look like the place he had left a few minutes previously. It was, he knew, the same: there was his bed, there was his lamp, the shoebox of gear, the stacks of CDs and flyers for the band, the bicycle frame he had lifted from a skip with the vague idea that he would, one day, fix it up into something he could ride. His keyboard was there, on its stand. But none of it looked familiar. Over everything— the floor, the bed, the CDs—were fragments of glass. In some places there were large shards; one had fallen into the groove between two floorboards and tilted upwards, jutting back at the branches where the window had been.

Billy picked his way towards the empty frame. Fragments of the pane remained at the edges in jagged chunks. Leaning out, he peered down. It was dark, and everything looked orange in the light cast by streetlamps. In the place where the tree had stood, there was a car, turned at an odd angle to the road. Its bonnet was crumpled. Half underneath it, where the trunk had been planted, a large hole gaped like a mouth. Roots were exposed, wriggling up between the vehicle's front wheels. The tree tilted diagonally from the pavement to Billy's window. People were standing in a circle around the scene; somebody pointed when Billy appeared and they all looked up.

"What the fuck," said Billy.

The driver was still in the car: a girl with a pale face and messy black hair. Her fingers were curled around the steering wheel. The people on the street had opened the car door and were trying to persuade her to move. After a moment, she turned and let a man scoop her out. She was skinny, Billy saw, once she was standing up, and for a second he thought it was Amy. He thought she had Amy's face, and Amy's thin wrists dangling from the sleeves of her sweater. He felt sick, then, and put a hand to his pocket to see if he had any pills on him. The pocket was empty.

It was only when the wind blew rain onto his face that he realized the people below were trying to get his attention. He blinked and rubbed the water out of his eyes.

"What?" he shouted.

The man who had lifted the girl from the car replied: "Are you all right, mate?"

Billy nodded.

"I've called an ambulance," the man said, "and the police."

Billy's nausea returned. The rain was cold. He glanced again at the girl who had been in the car. She was crying. She looked nothing like Amy.

He had grown so accustomed to the pang of loss each time this happened, each time he was forced to remind himself Amy was dead, that it was almost pleasurable. He let himself feel it for a second—the twist in his stomach—and then he began to move again. He ducked away from the window and began looking for his phone.

It was under his pillow, and he had to grope around through the broken glass before he felt it. He dialled Dave the Bass's number, cradling the mobile between his shoulder and his ear as he reached under the bed. It rang for a long time.

At last: "Billy Keys!" It was loud, wherever Dave the Bass was. A beat was thudding down the line, and there were voices in the background.

"Mate," said Billy.

"What's going on?"

It wasn't until he tried to form a sentence that Billy realized how high he was. He found the carrier bag he had been reaching for under the bed and pulled it out. Inside: an eighth of weed, a tiny bit of coke that some girl had left behind after his thirtieth months ago, and an air-rifle-pellet tin half full of ketamine. He twisted the bag closed again, lifted the lid of the shoebox and put it inside.

"Mate?" said Dave the Bass. "What's going on?"

The shoebox contained Billy's own things: his prescription Valium, a baggie of pills, some weed, and a novelty bong that had the words "Get High & Get Down in London Town" on the side. He fingered the Valium packet, counting the remaining tablets; there were nine. He knew that if he concentrated he would be able to work out how many he had taken that day, but he couldn't get a handle on the numbers, and instead leaned back, pushing the box away from him with his feet.

"A tree came through my window," said Billy. "The police are coming."

"Come over," said Dave the Bass. "We're having a shindig."

"Where are you?"

"My place."

Billy clenched his jaw. "I hate your fucking shindigs, Dave."

"Just come over. Make sure you don't leave anything."

"A tree came through my window."

"Just come over."

As Dave hung up, sirens sounded in the distance. The police would be streaming past Camden Town station; they would be outside the flat in less than a minute. Looking down, Billy realized blood was coming from somewhere, running along his wrist. He inspected his hands and found a cut on one of his knuckles. When he scratched it, a splinter of glass came loose.

With the shoebox tucked under his arm, Billy took the stairs two at a time and left the flat through the back door. He jogged towards the high street, keeping his head down. The contents of the box were rattling; he tried to carry it as though there were shoes inside. The rain intensified, and as water soaked through to his skin, his head cleared. He hadn't done anything wrong. It wasn't a crime to have a tree smash into your bedroom. It wasn't a crime to leave your own flat at high speed, carrying a shoebox. The police couldn't touch him for that.

The sound of the party reached him as he turned the corner onto Dave's road: music, voices. Dave's front door was half-open and he slipped through without touching it. When he surveyed the hallway, he was relieved to see that, for the most part, the people there were familiar: members of his band or other bands.

"Billy Keys!"

Dave was there, pushing through the cluster of people. A cigarette hung from his lips as he smiled. He thumped a hand on Billy's back.

"What's up with your face?"

"What?"

"You shaved off half your beard."

Billy put a hand to his chin. His stubble was patchy, rough in places and smooth where he had begun to shave before the crash. He shrugged. He opened his mouth to begin to explain about the tree, but Dave shouted across the room, "Billy's here! He's brought us a little party."

He meant the shoebox. Billy crouched down to open it, grabbed the carrier bag and held it out to Dave.

"That shit's yours," Billy said. "This is mine." He slid the lid back onto the box.

Dave took the bag. The other members of the band emerged from the crowd: Tom Bone and Rat and Boyd. Tom Bone, bronzed and muscular, a foot taller than everyone else, had hair that came down to his shoulders and always seemed to have girls attached to it, their fingers playing with its blonde ends, braiding and twisting it. Billy didn't recognize the one who was there now, clasping his elbow, but she looked like all the others. Her pupils were wide, and dark. Tom Bone's were the same. Billy smiled.

"Good time, Boney?" he asked.

Tom Bone shrugged as though trying to dislodge the girl from his arm. She clung fast. "Yeah," he said. "Good time."

"He's fucked up," said Dave.

"Everyone's fucked up," said Billy. "A tree just smashed through my window," he said, but none of the band seemed to hear.

Billy Keys, Dave the Bass, Tom Bone and Tom Bone's girl were together in the top-floor bathroom. Dave's house was large, four storeys high, and the party sounded distant from where they were, as though it had nothing to do with them. Billy had been drinking; he had taken a couple of pills. It was nearly morning. He could see the sky brightening through the window over the bath.

"So is it true that you knew Amy?"

He was sitting on the floor with his back to the wall, his legs pulled in towards his chest. His shoebox was tucked under his knees. The question drifted around him, and seemed at first as though it were one of his own thoughts.

Tom Bone, lying in the empty bath, extended a leg and kicked him in the thigh. He looked up.

"What, mate?"

"She's talking to you."

"Who's talking to me?"

"I am," said Tom Bone's girl.

As he stared at her, Billy remembered the face of the driver emerging from the crumpled car outside his flat. He blinked, and behind his eyelids he saw the shard of glass stuck in the floor of his room.

"Billy Keys?"

He squinted at the girl. Her features came into focus; she had taken off her glasses.

"Huh?"

"Is it true you knew Amy?"

Billy nodded.

"Uh-huh."

"How did you know her?"

Dave groaned.

Billy's tongue ran over the backs of his teeth. He was aware that he was smiling, his lips stretched across his face; he was also aware that the smile didn't reflect what he was feeling.

How did he know Amy?

He had been in the pub, sitting alone by the window. He remembered it as the same afternoon the girl who had once lived with him had packed her bags and disappeared, but it could have been another day, a different Tuesday, Wednesday, or Thursday, drizzle outside, a draught blowing in whenever someone came or went. He had been by himself and then somebody had flicked his shoulder.

"She just came up to me," he said.

He was speaking slowly; he knew there was a difference between the way he remembered it all, down to the sound of Amy's fingernail scraping the fabric of his jacket, and the way it came out of his mouth. The difference gaped, like the hole outside his flat where the tree's roots had been.

"She comes up to me and says, 'You're in my seat.'"

Her voice had carried across the whole bar. People had turned and stared.

"She says, 'You're in my seat,' and I get up and scurry away. I didn't even think about it."

"Fuck," said Tom Bone from the bath, "I just had the worst déjà vu. It's like I've heard this exact story before." He smacked himself in the face so hard that it left a pink stain on his cheek. "Oh, yeah, that's right. I have. A million fucking times."

"I had a whole stack of flyers with me on the table," said Billy. The words were coming more easily. He felt as though something had been holding him back, like a soft pedal on a piano, and that it had been lifted. "I was grabbing them together to leave and I dropped one and it sort of zigzags down to the floor, and she watches it fall and then stamps her foot on it, right on it, and says, 'Run along, little girl.'"

"Leave it, Billy," said Dave. Then, looking at the girl, he said, "Don't get him started."

When Billy next looked around, Dave the Bass and Tom Bone were gone. Tom Bone's girl was still there, sitting on the toilet.

They stared at each other in silence, Billy and the girl.

After a while, she said, "I'll listen to you."

"Huh?"

"I'm just saying—if you want to talk about Amy, I'll listen. Tom, Dave, they can be dicks sometimes."

The girl slid down from the toilet to join him on the floor. She reached out and brushed his knee with her fingers. The touch made his skin prickle. Her hand trailed up along his thigh and paused, trembling slightly, just below his groin.

"Take whatever you want from the box," he said. He slid it out from under his legs.

She opened it and began to sift through its contents with her free hand.

"I'll listen," she said again.

"A tree smashed through my window," he said, "and I don't know what the fuck to do about it."

He bent forward and pushed his face between his knees. He closed his eyes and when he opened them he could see the girl's hand trapped between his legs and stomach.

He wasn't expecting the reply, when it came. She was close to him; when she spoke he could hear the click of saliva between her lips.

"You should call your landlord, then."

He looked up and leaned back so that her hand was freed. Her fingers trailed across his crotch and hooked over the edge of his jeans.

"I went back," he said, "after that first time with Amy. I went back to the same pub, and I sat in the same seat, and waited. Do you ever—have you ever felt like that, like you just have something to do with someone, and they have something to do with you, and all you have to do is figure out what it is?"

The girl looked him in the eye when she answered him. "Yes."

He ignored the way she was staring.

"She was everywhere by then," he said. "In the papers. Everywhere. Famous. I went back and waited, night after night, and then one day she was there again. For some reason she remembered me."

"Of course she remembered you," said the girl. "You're Billy Keys."

Billy closed his eyes and tried to concentrate. He heard the crinkling of plastic. The girl was opening his baggie of pills.

"She comes up and says, 'If it isn't the little girl back in my seat,' and I straight out asked her if she'd record a track with our band. She laughed. She sat on the table and put her feet on my legs, and she was wearing these shoes with the heels, you know, the high heels, and they dug into my legs so hard I had bruises for weeks."

He had, once, after she died, pushed pens into his thighs to remember how it had felt.

"What she said—she said, 'You'll be OK, Billy Keys.' She looked right at me when she said it, and you wouldn't believe anyone else saying something pointless like that, but you sort of believed Amy, just for the moment when she was talking to you."

He felt the girl's lips touch his. He didn't do anything about it. She slid her hand inside his jeans. After a moment, Billy gripped her waist and guided her into his lap. His palm rested on the small of her back as she kissed him and ground her hips against his. Her mouth tasted of alcohol and fried food. He kissed her, but missed the story he had been telling. He missed the sound of his own voice.

She pushed hard against him and pulled back from his lips. "You'll be OK, Billy Keys," she said.

He had never spoken to Amy again, after that evening, but he had felt constantly on the alert, ready for their next meeting. Whenever the band played, he had scanned the audience for her face. He checked queues in supermarkets, at ATMs, in case she was there. He had seen her in clubs, but she had always been unreachable, surrounded by people with stronger claims to her than his. He had waved, once, and she had looked vague, then waved back. The glitter painted on her nails had caught the light; her hand had looked for a second as though it were dissolving.

He had been patient. He had waited for her.

"Hey," said Tom Bone's girl. She pushed her tongue into his mouth. She dug her hand further down inside his boxers. "Nothing's happening."

Billy's attention came back to the room and the girl straddling him. She was sweating; strands of her hair were stuck to her forehead. Her eyes, with their stretched pupils, were red, and the skin around them was grey. The smell of food on her breath made him feel ill. Then she bit him, hard, on the lip. He felt her teeth grind against the flesh.

Billy pushed her away and she slid onto the floor. Her head thudded against the toilet bowl and she let out a giggle.

"The papers said it was just alcohol," she murmured, without getting up, "that killed Amy. It was just alcohol?"

Billy's lip felt swollen where she had bitten him, and when he opened his mouth to reply, he spat.

"Misadventure," he said. "They called it a fucking misadventure."

Tom Bone's girl giggled again, but more quietly, and then went silent. Billy watched her for a while: the rising and falling of her breasts as she breathed, and her eyelids as they slid, slowly, over her eyes.

It had taken the coroner four months to declare the cause of Amy's death. The official announcement had been made only a week previously, and the word had been spinning around Billy's head ever since: misadventure. Death by misadventure. It was a term people found funny. Dave had roared with laughter and said, "Misadventure? I'll show you a fucking misadventure," before grabbing Rat's saxophone and thrusting his crotch at the bell, groaning and then miming an ejaculation that began low and rose until it exploded in Billy's face.

Billy woke up. His head was pounding and his tongue felt too big in his mouth. He was still curled against the bathroom wall, his knees pulled up towards him. The girl was lying on the mat. When he reached out and tilted his shoebox towards him, he found that the only thing left was the "Get High & Get Down" bong. He dropped the box and the sound of the bong sliding against the cardboard base made his skin crawl. His only clear thought was that he needed to go home.

He prodded the girl with his foot. Her leg wobbled where he had pushed it, but she didn't stir. Billy cleared his throat as loudly as he could. The pressure of the cough made his head spin. He didn't want to move. It would hurt him to move.

"Hey," he said, "girl?" His voice sounded explosive, as though he were underwater. "Tom Bone's girl?"

She didn't move. He hauled himself forwards, away from the wall, and crouched over her. She had been sick in her sleep; a trail of vomit had dried on her chin and a pool of it had soaked into the bath mat and caught in her hair. Her left arm was extended, as though reaching for something.

Billy staggered to his feet, gripping the toilet to steady himself. This was how she must have looked, he thought: when Amy died, she had been alone, and drunk, and this must have been how she looked.

He turned away, and let his forehead fall against the wall. He was breathing heavily, and each time he inhaled, his head pressed harder into the plaster and throbbed. Then he pushed himself upright and ran out of the room, down the four flights of stairs and out of the front door.

It had stopped raining, but only recently. The roads were still wet, reflecting the headlights of traffic. A bus passed and sent up a spray of water from a flooded drain. Billy didn't look at the people he ran past, or the cars, or the drivers in the cars.

When he reached the high street, he dug in his pocket for his phone, found the 9 at the bottom-left corner of the keypad, and pressed it three times.

"Which emergency service do you require?"

"I don't know," said Billy. His words came out garbled. "I don't know. Someone's died. Someone's died. There's a dead girl."

He just kept saying it until the operator redirected his call. He spoke first to paramedics, and then to the police. He gave them his name, his address, and Dave's name and Dave's address, and a description of where the girl was in the house. When they asked him where he was at that moment, he just said, "I don't know, I don't know," and stared at the red-and-blue sign for the Tube station.

"I gave her the drugs," he said. "I gave them to her, and I didn't even look at what she was taking, and then she didn't wake up, and I just ran away."

"You need to calm down, Billy," said the voice on the other end of the phone. Billy ended the call.

Inside the Tube station, people were passing through the barriers, vanishing down escalators. Some of them were smiling, as though nothing were wrong. He paced between the wall and a stand advertising planned line closures for the weekend. He called Dave the Bass.

"Billy Keys." He could tell from the tone of Dave's voice that he was lying down.

"Dave the Bass."

"Where are you?"

"I just left your place."

"You have a good time last night, Billy?"

"That girl, that girl—Tom Bone's girl—is dead. She fucking died. I've called the police. I've called an ambulance."

"What?"

"Go upstairs," said Billy. "She's dead. I just ran. I shouldn't have run. There's an ambulance coming."

"What?" said Dave the Bass. "Who are you talking about? Gina? That girl Gina that was with Tom Bone?"

"The girl that was with us in the bathroom."

"Oh, my God," said Dave. "Gina. Where is she?"

"In the bathroom," said Billy. "In the bathroom where we all were."

Billy could hear thudding footsteps and Dave's heavy breathing as he ran to the top of the house.

"Fuck, fuck, fuck," Dave said under his breath.

"I gave her pills," said Billy. "I don't know what she had, but nothing was left in the box when I woke up. Nothing."

Dave continued to run, and then there was a silence. Billy imagined him standing in the bathroom doorway, staring at the body of the girl.

Dave said nothing.

"Dave?" said Billy.

"I'm in the bathroom."

"What are we going to do?" said Billy. "I don't know what the fuck is going to happen."

"Mate, she's not here."

"In the bathroom," Billy said. "The bathroom. The mat by the toilet."

"She's not here."

Down the phone, Billy could hear sirens growing louder.
After a moment, they were so loud that Dave was shouting over
the noise.

"What the fuck, Billy? What the fuck?"

"She's there," Billy said. He couldn't think clearly. "She's dead
on the mat."

The sirens stopped. People were shouting in Dave's house.
The doorbell rang. There were more raised voices, another
shrill ring, heavy footsteps. Dave hung up.

The year before, it had been Tom Bone, of all people, who had
called.

"Mate, where are you?" Tom Bone had said. He was speaking
so clearly that at first Billy thought one of the others was using
Tom's phone. "Something's happened. Something's happened
to Amy."

"What's happened?" Billy asked.

"Turn on the news."

"What's happened?"

There was a pause and then Tom Bone said, "I think she's
died."

Billy had run the entire distance from the Twelve Bar on
Denmark Street to Camden Square. The sole had come loose
on his left shoe and smacked against the pavement with
each step. It had sounded like applause. When he reached
the square, crowds were pushing against a line of police. He
elbowed his way past sobbing teenagers, journalists with micro-
phones, and tourists holding up cameras.

Once he reached the front, he had a clear view of the white
wall in front of Amy's house, the fortified black gate and the
police cordon around it. He stood with the crowd, waiting for

something to happen. He waited for hours. Nothing happened. She was already gone.

Billy's phone didn't stop ringing as he walked towards Camden Square. He felt it buzzing in his pocket for minutes on end, and then the battery died.

Outside the house that had once been Amy's, a police officer was standing guard. Billy walked along the wall in front of the building. People still left flowers there, and other things: cups of coffee that got kicked over so that the pavement was awash with soured milk and brown puddles; cigarettes; bottles of booze.

He crouched down and stared at the pavement between his feet. When he tried to focus on the situation with Tom Bone's girl, his brain froze and all he could think about was Amy. He wanted Amy. Wind and drizzle rushed through the trees in the park across the road: a hissing sound like suppressed laughter.

The police officer's hand on his shoulder made him jump. He looked up into the woman's face.

She was frowning. "You OK?"

She was trying to look into his eyes. Billy glared at his knees.

"Important to you, was she?" said the woman.

Something about the word "important" made tears spring into Billy's eyes. He heard the woman move off, and the clink of glass a few feet away. He looked across, then, and saw her take two bottles of whisky from the cluster of gifts by the house.

She walked back to him and held them out. "Here."

He wiped his face with the insides of his wrists. He didn't move to take them.

"Safe to say your need is greater than hers," she said.

She put the bottles into his hands. The glass was cold; the

whisky sloshed inside. He slid them into the inner pockets of his jacket, one on each side.

"Now get on home, have a drink, and sleep it off," said the policewoman. "You'll be OK."

The tree outside Billy's flat was gone. The hole in the pavement was cordoned off with yellow tape. Billy's front door was ajar. He inspected the door frame. The paintwork was scratched where someone had forced the lock.

He pushed his head through the gap and called up the stairs. "Hello?"

"Mate?" said a voice. "Billy?"

"Who is that?"

There was no answer. Billy stepped inside, kicked the door shut and ran upstairs. His head throbbed with the effort. His vision was spinning as he stepped into his room.

Tom Bone was sitting amongst broken glass on the bed. The room and all the furniture looked smaller beside his bulk. It was dark. He hadn't turned on the light, and the normal orange glow of the streetlamps outside was absent. The window had been covered with a black bin liner, stuck to the walls with police tape.

Billy flicked the light switch and Tom Bone raised a hand to shade his eyes. He had sheets of paper in his lap and envelopes that had been torn open.

"The police were here," Tom Bone said, waving the letters, "because of the tree. They forced entry in case there were casualties. Your landlord came and changed the locks—he stuck a note to the front door because you weren't answering your phone. You can go and collect the new key from him."

Billy nodded. His eyes turned to the glass on the floor, the twigs and leaves the tree had left behind, and then back to his friend.

"How did you get in?"

"I fucking kicked the door until it opened."

Tom Bone laughed and looked around as though searching for someone other than Billy who could share the joke. He clenched his fists, then laid his palms flat on his thighs. Billy sat next to him. Pieces of glass clattered as the mattress sank under his weight. He slid one of the bottles of whisky out of his pocket and handed it to Tom Bone.

Tom Bone twisted the cap off, and tilted the bottle into his mouth. A trickle of liquid slid out of the corner of his lips.

"So we're all at Dave's," said Tom Bone, after a silence. He wiped his chin on his sleeve. "Everyone's waking up, feeling like shit. But we're all right. We had a good time."

Billy opened the other bottle and drank.

"Then we hear the sirens. They're getting louder and Dave is yelling on the phone at the top of the house. The doorbell rings. Dave goes, 'It's the police, it's the fucking police.' People are going mental, flushing everything they can find, but it's pointless, because everything was everywhere. The police are in the house. The fucking paramedics are there, yelling, 'Where's the girl? Where's the girl?' and people are running around trying to find the corpse that was supposed to be in the top bathroom but wasn't, and eventually the doctors are like, 'Is this a joke? Are you wasting our time?' and then Gina bursts into the room going, 'We've searched everywhere and nobody's dead. Everybody's fine.'"

"You don't mean Gina," Billy said. "You mean someone else."

Tom Bone ignored him. "And I'm just staring, staring at her, and nobody says anything for fucking ages, and then Dave goes,

'It's you, though. It's you. You're supposed to be dead. Billy Keys told us you were dead.' And she says it again—she says, 'Nobody's dead.'" Tom Bone's hands were trembling around the bottle. Inside, the brown liquid shivered.

"'Nobody's dead,'" Billy repeated. He stamped on a fragment of glass on the floor. He felt it splinter through the sole of his shoe.

"She was fine. Hungover as hell, but we all were."

Billy nodded. It was hard to stop nodding. He felt his jaw wobbling as his head moved.

"So it's OK," he said. "It's all OK."

"Meanwhile," said Tom Bone, "the police barge into the room asking whose house it is. Dave holds up his hand and his face is white. They charge him on the spot with possession with intent, and he just sighs. They cuff him. Off they go."

Billy was still nodding. "OK," he said. "OK. But you're OK. They let you go."

"I came round here and I wanted to fucking kill you, Billy, for the spectacular shit you just pulled. But then I sat here and I waited and I looked around at all your stuff covered in glass, and I realized that's not why I came—not to hit you, mate. You have fucked up, Billy, and part of me still wants to smash this bottle in your fucking face, but I wanted to see you before— before—to tell you that I—that we –" Tom Bone stopped and took a long swig of whisky—"that mates stand by mates."

Billy put a hand to his own forehead. He rubbed the skin. "Gina, how old is she?" he said.

Tom Bone began to say, "Sixtee—" but before he could finish the word, he leaned forward and threw up. The muscles of his back churned as he retched. The vomit covered their shoes and seeped over the broken glass. It splashed onto Billy's legs.

The sharp smell of alcohol and bile burned in his nose when he inhaled.

"So the police are coming here, then?" said Billy. "They're on their way?"

Tom Bone was still bent double. His hair had fallen forward and was covering his face. He nodded and almost at once the banging started at the door.

Four Photographs of My Face

When you live in a small and constant world, and the view from your window every morning is the same patch of moss and rocks and water and sky, and the Internet is slow, expensive, and normally down—when you have lived alone on Bleaker Island for fifty-six sachets of powdered soup and 60,000 words—little changes become big news.

The weather is a soap opera: the wind is in the west! The south! The south-west! It's snowing. The snow is melting. Snow is falling again.

The caracaras have eaten one of the hens! There are glossy green-black feathers strewn all around the coop, and further off, in the grass, a pink and flimsy skeleton.

Sometimes the little red planes fly overhead—occasionally there are larger military aircraft too—and I stare up at them, gaping, until my mouth gets filled with sleet. Soon George and

Alison will be back, marking the beginning of the end of my time on the island, and the anticipation of this feels almost ominous, though I don't know exactly why.

My body is becoming unfamiliar. It is a garden turning wild. Things expand. Things contract. The bulges and wobbles of fat with which I have, in recent years, made an uneasy truce, are gradually deserting me. Underneath: a rougher, leaner person.

These are the assumptions under which I have been labouring: that if I spend long enough on Bleaker Island, if I spend enough time entirely alone, my own true self will be revealed to me; that I will strip away all but the essentials of myself and discover within a kind of authentic core; that finding that core will be good, and solid, and healthy, and strong, and will make me a better writer.

I think about the night before I left London and the words of my friend the actor, the note of doubt in her voice as she said, "Perhaps you know yourself quite well already?" How well did I know myself then? Do I know myself better now? I wanted to find out everything about myself: not just the profound and often boring things to do with childhood memories and self-respect, but also the practical stuff, like what my first book will actually be about. I assumed I would have discovered all of these things by now.

Related to this assumption, albeit tangentially, was the belief that by doing nothing, or as little as possible, in the way of personal grooming, I would arrive at a kind of physical equilibrium, an entirely natural state, which might not be beautiful but which would nonetheless feel somehow "right." My physical changes would run parallel to my emotional and literary ones, so that, by the time I left the island, I would take off in the little red plane as a coherent and robust identity: a body, brain and book that all made sense in relation to each other.

My concessions to grooming have consisted of soap, shampoo, moisturizer, a nail file, deodorant and sunblock. When I write it out it seems as though it should be plenty— not much of an achievement, in fact, to live without anything else—and yet without tweezers, without conditioner, hand cream, lip balm, a foot file, the stony-faced woman at the salon who shapes and buffs my nails, or the girl with the soft voice who tries to make waxing seem like a luxury experience, I become foreign to myself. My hands are excruciating, dry, raw, cuticles a mess of cracks and tears. I measure out moisturizer as carefully as I do my daily ration of almonds, trying to make it last and last. My eyebrows, which were somewhat over-pruned by a threader in Boston on my final visit, are now so thick and unruly they resemble my grandfather's. My legs and underarms first turned prickly and are now exuberantly furry. The skin on my feet has become so hard that I sleep in socks to stop my heels grating against the sheets.

I do not feel that I have become a truer version of myself. I could deal with the body hair, I think, but not the eyebrows, which are now so distracting that I have to cover the mirror hanging by the door of the sunroom. I don't really mind the bushy, knotted, unconditioned tangle of hair on my head, but the pain of my dry lips, splitting heels and torn fingernails surprises me.

There is no natural point to which I can return. There is only a variety of states, each one as peculiar as the others.

Though I've covered the mirror in the sunroom, where I write, I allow myself unrestricted access to the one in my bedroom.

It is comforting, when I wake up, to see the movement of my reflection. It looks so strange and unfamiliar, it is almost as though there were someone else there. At the end of the day I often find myself standing immobile in front of the glass, scrutinizing my own image; sometimes I stare for so long I no longer recognize myself at all.

I become obsessed in a way I know is not healthy with a small patch of skin beside my top lip. It is pink, slightly flaky. I use valuable Internet time looking up what it is: cancer, the Internet tells me, at once. You have cancer.

The reasonable part of me is dubious of this diagnosis, but without anyone to talk me out of my neurosis, my paranoid self takes charge. I layer so much sunblock onto this particular patch of skin that, as time passes, I'm not sure whether the mark I can see is the original, or simply a reaction to all the sunblock I've put on it.

Offensive, too: the asymmetrical slant of my nose, broken when I was a toddler. It is flabbergasting to me that I have had this odd, tilted, dissatisfying nose almost my entire life and have only just noticed it. The unnatural angle appears so outrageous, so disfiguring, that I'm suddenly unsure how I have functioned in society until now.

My face, under scrutiny, looks as though it has been assembled by a child in nursery school: one eye higher than the other, one brow raised and the other flat, the nose swerving off to the side.

I am not a symmetrical person. I am a wonky person.

I am a wonky person with face cancer.

I take four photographs of my face at two-week intervals. Juxtaposed, the pictures chart a woman going to seed. The eyebrows thicken. The cheeks sink. Freckles creep across the nose. Most noticeable, though, are the eyes that get wider and glassier each time. In the final photograph, taken the week before George and Alison are due to return, what strikes me more than the newly emerged cheekbones, more than the pale, watery eyes, more than the flaking lips, is how young I look. It is as though I have fallen backwards into myself. I could be eighteen in the photograph, I think—or at least, I could be eighteen if, as a child, I had been lost on the moor and had spent a decade wandering through the elements, trying to find my way home.

I spend increasing amounts of time worrying about these things. Then I worry about time—about wasting it worrying about my appearance when what really matters is my work. The answer comes, always the same: just write your goddamn book. I have somehow fallen behind with my words, so that I can no longer use the rising counter at the bottom of my laptop screen as an accurate marker of time passing. I need to catch up.

Stop looking in the mirror. Stop loitering in the kitchen staring longingly at the potato. Stop applying disturbing amounts of sunblock. Write the book.

A Thirty-Minute Window

Beirut is dusty, lovely, and, for me, entirely new. I have completed my first year at university and have come here for a different kind of education. It is summer, dusk, and chokingly hot. I wander along the corniche, through long shadows thrown by palm trees, inhaling the salty breeze off the ocean. A soft, steady hum of conversation and piano music drifts up from restaurants that line the shore.

I have come to Lebanon with a group of students to teach English in a Palestinian refugee camp for the summer months. We are spending an orientation week together in Beirut before dispersing around the country; I will be going to a camp called Rashidieh, in the south, near the border with Israel, which I have requested specifically because it is the birthplace of Samir el-Youssef. *Gaza Blues*, el-Youssef's story collection, written jointly with Israeli writer Etgar Keret, is one of the reasons I wanted to come. In my imagination, the camp, perched on the

Mediterranean coast, is both sublime and horrifying: half literary idyll, half violent, impoverished prison.

My predominant feeling about the experience, however, is not excitement, or fear, or homesickness, but anxiety. And what I am anxious about is not the risk of kidnap, or being caught in crossfire, or being blown up by a terrorist at a checkpoint, which is what the safety briefings before we left tried to focus our attention on. What I am anxious about is standing in front of a class of children at the summer school and having to teach them something. My dreams are a series of classroom-based disaster movies: there are floods, fires, children metamorphosing into various predators. In one, I am trying to teach the students to say "My name is," but instead they repeat, in unison, the phrase "No man's land," over and over.

I have a suitcase full of colouring books and games and felt-tip pens, a syllabus supplied by the organization that arranged the trip, and a pressing awareness of how ill-equipped I am, at twenty, to teach anyone anything. I wish I could stay in Beirut indefinitely, and that Rashidieh and the summer school could remain forever on the horizon, suspended in the warm air beyond the piano music and the breeze.

I stray from the corniche. I eat ice cream and honey-drenched confectionery in glassy, marble-floored parlours, and take pictures of buildings scarred by bullets shot in long-ago battles. On our first evening, the group gathers on the roof of the hotel. People smoke self-consciously and strum guitars, also self-consciously. Below us on the street, a parade of young men on motorbikes roars past, waving acid-yellow flags and firing guns at the sky.

. . .

The next day I wake to discover that, as we have been sleeping, a war has broken out. Hezbollah has captured two Israeli soldiers. In retaliation, Israel has begun to shell Beirut. The group of student volunteers gathers around the television in the hotel lobby, taking turns to sit near the small, noisy fan that churns up hot air. All day, no one goes outside. The hotel owner's daughter brings us bags of pastries, grease soaking through the brown paper. I am worried, sorry and alarmed, but also can't help thinking that, if this means our trip might be cancelled, I won't have to teach in the summer school after all. I call my parents from the payphone behind the front desk. When my father suggests that everything will blow over in a day or so, I am both comforted and, shamefully, more anxious again.

I fall asleep under a sheet that is soaked with sweat. When I wake the next day and look out of the window, the city is still there. Nothing appears to be burning. I am alive. War is over, I think. My father was right.

When I join the group gathered around the television in the lobby, I learn that, overnight, the Israelis have bombed the airport. Up to this point, the conflict has been alarming but somehow, in spite of the proximity of the falling shells, distant. Suddenly, now, it is real. The airport, where we landed three days ago with our cases full of toys and pens and school supplies, is gone from the earth, and we are stuck. In an instant, the city shrinks to the size of this sweaty room.

We escape in a yellow van driven by strangers. At first, it proves almost impossible to find anyone willing to risk the trip; the Arabic speakers in our group spend the morning wandering the streets around the hotel, asking after drivers. Eventually, they find three willing, excitable young men, who arrive at the hotel two hours later. In the lobby, they waste no time with introductions, and hurry us outside into their vehicle. Together, we begin our long journey out of the city.

Inside the van, there are not enough seats, so we are piled in haphazardly, sitting on each other's laps or on the floor on people's feet. The neck of somebody's guitar juts into my back. As we drive, I watch Beirut outside the window: flashes of blue water between buildings, a pile of smouldering rubble, the aftermath of a bomb dropped in the night. The road is so dusty that the driver flicks on the wipers, carving clear arcs through a beige haze. We are speeding, careering around corners and over bumps and divots in the road. When we thud across a pothole, one of the boys in our group grunts his disapproval. At this, the driver turns his eyes from the road—though he does not slow down—peering into the rearview mirror to look at us and shout, by way of explanation, "Quickly, quickly."

Once we reach the outskirts of the city, the roads even out and the van slows down. One of the men pushes a tape into the cassette player. Music begins to crackle through the speakers. I don't listen closely; I'm still trying to see outside, although by now the windows are heavily smeared with grime.

"Sing!" one of the men says. He starts to croon along to the tape and clap his hands. When nobody joins him, he says, more forcefully, "Sing now."

None of us knows the tune. It is complicated and hard to follow. The noise we produce as a group is more of a drone than a song—there's one moment, which must be the chorus, that is clearer than the rest, and I sing that more loudly until one of the other girls, an Arabic speaker called Sara, whispers in my ear, "You know what you're singing, right?"

"No, what is it?"

Before Sara answers, I know what she will say. I realize that, although I know no Arabic, the word I've been happily singing for the past few minutes is familiar to me. The word is "Hezbollah."

"The song is saying," Sara whispers, "'One Hezbollah for the whole world. One God for the whole world. Hezbollah will rule the whole world. Hezbollah, Hezbollah, Hezbollah . . .'"

Whenever our volume drops, the men at the front turn and shout, "Sing!" as if our voices are powering the van. Then we start up again, raucously chanting joyful allegiance to a terrorist organization.

The men drop us in Byblos, a small Christian town by the sea. Our plan is to stay here at a distance from the violence and await rescue. It is a holiday resort, but deserted. We have the stony beach to ourselves. We float and paddle in the shallows, sharing a sense of overwhelming relief, though none of us ever admits to having been scared. Those nights in Beirut and the chaotic journey out of the city offered a glimpse of a new sort of reality—serious, sinister, powerful—that now, in the bright sunlight of the empty town, recedes like the tide.

We are waiting for instructions. The director of the organization in London is trying to arrange help for us. Until this is finalized, there is nothing to do. At night, down the coast, we can see Beirut. It is a constellation of lights, as peaceful and remote as the stars overhead. From above, we hear the drone of planes on their way to drop bombs.

At some point, a collective decision is made that the formal part of the programme is officially over, which means the organization's rules banning its volunteers from having alcohol no

longer apply. We drink beer on the roof of the hotel and spend
our evenings in a vague, mirthful haze.

The people who eventually come to rescue us work for an
organization called International SOS. They are muscular,
severe, ex-military men who specialize in evacuating civilians
from conflict situations. They have been in Afghanistan and
Chechnya, but they seem taken aback by the task of shepherd-
ing a group of politically principled but immature students
from a deserted seaside resort across the border into Syria.

The man in charge is called Rob. He has a moustache and
never smiles. He likes to bark everything he says, even "Good
morning!" and "Has anyone seen my sunglasses!" Shortly after
pulling up outside our hotel in Byblos, he tells us to pack our
things. We will be leaving in twenty minutes' time to drive to
the Syrian border. We can't afford to be late. Three-quarters
of an hour later, we are all inside the black International SOS
van, and Rob is red-faced, sweating, and furious. "I said twenty
minutes!" he shouts. "Twenty minutes! I said don't be late. You
were late!"

We begin to drive, and the group lapses into a sheepish
silence. We are heading away from the coast, inland, and as we
go on the landscape starts to look bleaker and darker. By the
time we reach the border, the atmosphere inside the vehicle
has turned tense and moody. Outside, there are large crowds of
people milling around a checkpoint, waiting to cross over into
Syria. Rob ushers us off the bus. We file down the steps towards
a concrete booth, where we present our passports to a man who
stamps them without checking them and keeps gazing distractedly up at an indeterminate point in the sky.

Somebody asks if there's a toilet nearby, and a few of the girls
wander off in search of one. A boy drags his guitar out of the

back of the van and starts strumming the chords of "Hey Jude." Sara and I decide to walk a little way back down the road to try to get a picture of the queue of people waiting to cross.

We hear Rob before we see him. His barking has turned into screaming: "Get on the bus! Get on the bus! Get on the bus!" We start to run. In response to his shouting and our panic, the crowd of other people waiting to cross starts to run too, and soon we are part of a stampede. Panting, Sara and I reach the group. We are the last two to reassemble. As I scramble up the steps and the door closes behind me, a woman thrusts something into my arms. It's a baby, squirming and pink-faced, and I howl at the driver to stop, to open the door again, so I can push the infant back out into the crowd, into somebody's hands.

We drive through the night, and by the time we reach Damascus it is nearly dawn. There is a sleepy gasp from the group as we near the city, the lights growing wider and brighter as we approach. We arrive at a large government building somewhere, and are given papers confirming our status as diplomatic refugees by a young British woman with a gratingly crisp accent. We sleep beside strangers in rows of folding beds in a large hall that has been repurposed to accommodate us.

In the morning, Rob wakes us with pastries. He is a changed man, smiling, urging us to eat.

"Listen, guys," he says, in his new mellow voice, "I'm sorry I was tough on you back there. But it was a tight situation. We bought a window from the Israelis, and it looked like we might miss it."

It takes some pleading to persuade Rob to explain this to us, but eventually he relents. International SOS had negotiated a thirty-minute window with the Israeli military, he says, during which time there would be no shelling of the border. We had been so slow, and so embarrassingly disorganized, playing guitar and taking photographs, that we had almost missed our slot.

"Why didn't you tell us?" someone asks.

"It's easier to herd stupid people than scared people," Rob says.

Two days later I have been repatriated and I am standing in my bedroom in my parents' house in Oxford. Objects that used to be familiar—trinkets from childhood, books from university— strike me now as foreign and strange. Everything looks incredibly clean. When I open my suitcase, felt-tip pens spill out onto the floor. I unpack untaught lesson plans, uncoloured colouring books, and my copy of *Gaza Blues*.

I attend a Stop the War rally in London. I feel a self-righteous investment in being there, in speaking out against a conflict that I sense I had something to do with. I imagine it will be cathartic, to walk through the city and shout about it. I hope it might help to mitigate the guilt I now feel about how unquestioningly I took my place in the International SOS van, leaving behind the hordes of other people massing at the border; how instantly I pushed that baby back out into the throng.

I surface from the Underground at Embankment, where the protest is already under way. The air is thick with the smells of weed and booze. People are drumming, singing, getting high. I walk along with them for a while: a woman with green hair twirling poi over her head; a family with three young girls whose faces are painted with Palestinian flags; an old man marching grimly with an accordion under his arm. Somewhere behind me, a chant starts up. At first, it is quiet, muffled. Then it is clear: "We are all Hezbollah! We are all Hezbollah!" The crowd picks up the mantra and repeats and repeats it. Beside us, the Thames is silvery and silent. "We are all Hezbollah!" the marchers shout. "We are all Hezbollah!"

I duck away from the flow of people and stand, instead, by the river.

Apples

am about to think something unthinkable, a chain of ideas that I now realize has been slowly forming for a while—*I may not be able to write this book*—when the plane arrives.

I hear it approaching the island and listen for a while before realizing what it is: a distant whirring, growing louder. Then, the aircraft appears in my line of vision, not just passing by but getting closer, larger, descending. It is going to land on Bleaker.

I am not expecting George and Alison back for another few days, and can think of no other reason why a plane would come to the island. I scramble into coat, hat, gloves and boots and start to run towards the airstrip, tripping in the boggy mud. The plane has landed and is out of sight over the crest of the hill, but I jog in the direction of the little flag marking the terminal hut, flapping in the wind. The cold air turns my throat raw. By the time I arrive at the airstrip, I am gasping. I bend over, hands on knees, and catch my breath.

The plane is crouching on the airstrip like a giant insect, bright red, alien-looking. For a second I am so staggered by it that I stay bent over, panting and staring. Then a door opens and the pilot steps out and shouts, "Nell?" into the wind.

"Hi," I say. "Yes, hi." The pilot is still staring expectantly, which makes me think that either I haven't spoken loud enough to be heard over the weather, or haven't actually spoken at all. "Hi," I try again, and then, inspired by the sight of the painted sign on the hut, "Welcome!," I am so anxious not to seem weird, not to appear too much like a person who has had nothing but birds for company for the past few weeks, that I am probably overcompensating.

The pilot is holding something. I stumble closer: it is a bag of apples.

"From Alison," he says, handing them over.

Though I have by now adjusted to the reduced calories of my island diet, and my days are no longer dominated by hunger pangs, it has nonetheless continued to encroach on my sanity and subconscious. Instant porridge, powdered soups, granola bars; nearly everything I eat comes in a little foil-lined sachet, and my dreams have started to feature a world in which everything—people, conversation—comes in a little foil-lined sachet. Now, confronted with apples, dangling weightily in a translucent plastic bag, rustling in the gale, I am overwhelmed. There is a beat before I take them from the pilot and stutter thanks. Alison's potato is still sitting untouched in the kitchen in the house, awaiting an emergency, but there are eight apples in the bag, and I have ten days left on Bleaker, and that means I can safely eat them without regret, starting the day after tomorrow. There's a note inside the bag: "Thought you might fancy something fresh. See you soon! A x."

Inside the plane there are two passengers: a doctor doing her rounds, flying settlement to settlement, and a Danish scientist who is bound for Sea Lion Island. The pilot introduces us and I wave awkwardly through the glass, wondering if I seem as strange to them as they do to me and concluding quickly that I must seem stranger: a solitary, wild-haired woman reduced almost to tears by a bag of fruit.

The pilot gets back inside the plane, then reappears at once. "Nearly forgot," he says. "There's this too."

He produces a large, battered white parcel, hands it over, and closes the door. I clutch it and watch as the plane accelerates, takes off and shrinks to the size of an albatross, a dark spot against darker clouds that look saggy now, full of snow.

The plane is suddenly gone and I am left standing alone at the airstrip, clutching the apples and the parcel as indisputable proof that what has just happened was real, was not a hallucination.

Every element of the island I encounter in my day-to-day life has become crushingly familiar to me: the view from the sunroom, the clothes I wear, the objects I handle, the different kinds of clouds. It has been a long time since I last saw something new. Just the sight of these unexpected objects is thrilling. The bruised red skins of the apples nestle together in the bag, dusty around the stalks. The parcel, scuffed and crinkled, has American stamps. It has been directed, in black ink, to the hotel in Stanley, but must have arrived after I left, since someone has crossed out the old address and written instead, "Nell Stevens, BLEAKER." I wonder who did that—Maura, perhaps? On the back is the name and address of my novelist friend in Boston.

Fat grey circles spatter across the paper. A dark curtain of rain is heading my way. I tuck the new possessions inside my coat and begin to move back towards the settlement.

As I walk, I entertain ludicrous fantasies about what might be inside the parcel: pasta, maybe, or rice. Part of me wants to linger, to draw out the novelty of not knowing what has suddenly arrived on the island. It could be something useful, like fresh notebooks, free from the messy scribbles I've dashed across the ones I brought. It could be something gloriously indulgent and pointless: a scented candle, a pair of earrings. Each of these successive thoughts delights me more than the last.

Back at the house, I manage to delay opening the package by insisting to myself that I need to shower first. Once clean, I take out the apples one by one and arrange them beside the potato. Then I make coffee, using tomorrow's ration since I've already had my day's share. I take the cup to the sunroom, where I sit, parcel in my lap, and prepare myself to be amazed.

Inside: an encouraging card from my novelist friend depicting an elderly woman flying a tiny plane and quoting Helen Keller—"Life is either a daring adventure or nothing"—and sheaths of CDs which glint and reflect the light in clear white rings. I slide a disc out and run my finger around its edge. Each one is like a whole new parcel: blank packaging and no hint as to what is inside. I have been sent a series of mysteries.

The house has a CD player, thankfully, and I feed it a disc at random. Outside, it has started to snow in broad, damp flakes that splatter on the roof of the sunroom, blocking out the last of the light. Then, from the speakers, the sound of an audience clapping. "This is a story," says a voice, twangy, American, "of the first time I hung out with Kanye West." It is Aziz Ansari, I realize, doing stand-up. There is laughter in the auditorium.

I glance around the room, searching for someone to thank. I don't know exactly what I am feeling, but I know that right now I wish there were a person here to share this surging, singing, surprised sensation.

"Thank you," I say, to the emptiness in the house.

Was it only a few hours ago that I almost-but-not-quite thought that awful thought about not being able to finish the book? Since then, the plane has arrived, and I met the pilot and the doctor and the sea-lion scientist, and Aziz Ansari has appeared in the sunroom and so much has happened in one day—The wind is in the west! The caracaras have eaten one of the hens! And a parcel! And apples!—that an unsettling and entirely new concern flits into my mind: what if, after all this time spent worrying about if and how I'm coping on the island, the reverse problem occurs? After these silent, windswept weeks alone, how will I readjust to the constant happenings and variousness of normal life? What will I make, now, of a London street, where thousands of people will do thousands of things, and the view will change, and buses will go by?

Putting the Girls Through

Three days later, Alison and George are back. I hear the sound of the plane approaching the island, its strange juddering, and a quarter of an hour later see the jeep they left at the airstrip rolling over the crest of the hill towards the settlement, past my house to theirs.

For some reason, my heart is pounding. I feel suddenly self-conscious and invaded. Whatever might have gone on since I last shared the island with other people, whatever difficulties I might have had with myself, with the book, it has all been private. Nobody has witnessed any of it and that has made it feel, if not less real, then at least less consequential. Now, I am faced with the prospect of having to account for how I have spent the past few weeks to the two people who know the island better than anyone. They have made it their home. It is completely ordinary to them. Any attempt on my part to explain my struggles with caracaras and dry heel skin and achieving the straightforward daily task of doing my words will surely strike George and Alison as melodramatic.

I have a week left on the island. By now, according to the original plan, I should have completed a draft and be luxuriating in the comparatively easy task of editing it. Instead, there are thousands of words more to write, and, worse, as I endeavour to get to the end of it, there will now be witnesses.

When Alison arrives outside the house, pulling up in her four-by-four and waving through the window, I find I am grateful for the brief exchange I had with the pilot days before, stilted as it might have been. I feel less rusty now than I otherwise would have. He reminded me what it was like to speak to another human being. I go out to greet Alison feeling moderately confident that I can at least hold my own in a conversation.

I try to look self-assured, breezy, as though I have nothing to hide. It takes me a moment to realize that I don't actually have anything to hide.

"Hop in," says Alison, with no preamble. "I'll take you to have a look at the North End."

The North End. I think at once of Boston, suddenly seeing, quite clearly, its narrow streets and Italian restaurants and the line of people stretching out of the door of Mike's pastry shop, waiting for cannoli. In Boston it is summer, and hot, and people will be eating seafood by open windows and drinking cold beer. The nostalgia is like a punch, and it takes a second for me to recover, to set my face into a smile.

She means the north end of the island, beyond the beach and the penguins, beyond even Big Pond, where I have sometimes gone to watch the black swans drift over the black water. The North End is far enough away that I have never reached it. We drive together into new territory, stopping occasionally so that Alison can jump out and plant tufts of tussac she has brought with her. The island gets so battered by the wind, she explains, that it is at risk of being blown away entirely: the more tussac she plants, the better chance the ground stands of holding together. We drive over flat, dark soil, not like the muddy, mossy ground of most of the island; it looks like the site of a huge fire. Alison points to flaking tubes of dark rock on the ground: these are the fossils of trees. Thousands of years ago, there was a forest on Bleaker.

The North End, when we get there, is a sharp, craggy point, black cliffs over kelp-slimed caves. There are wide holes in the rocks that give a view of the ocean churning underneath us; it makes me feel sick to look down, as though I am peering into an open stomach. Overhead, birds swerve across clouds; they are everywhere around us: in crannies, long grasses, squawking as they launch from the rocks. Alison points and names them as we scramble down to a stony beach littered with driftwood, and I nod as though I've heard of them before: variable hawk, giant petrel, black-crowned night heron. As the afternoon wears on, words gradually come back to me and I begin to participate in the conversation, the wind blowing gulps of salt into my mouth as I speak.

Alison asks how my novel is going, and I try to think of a reply that is honest without sounding forlorn: I haven't got as far with it as I'd like, I say. Sometimes it has been a little hard to do all my words. But still, I've nearly finished it now.

At the end of the beach, where mossy whale bones jut out of the ground, we climb back up the rocks to reach the very tip of Bleaker Island. East Falkland is ahead of us, disrupting the sweep of the horizon, vast and far away. I try to picture it as it is shown on the map—Bleaker a tiny comma off the coast of the mainland, itself a full stop marking the end of South America, the beginning of Antarctica—and feel suddenly dizzy, as though at any moment this flimsy little island might give way, and Alison and George and I, and the jeep and the houses and all the carefully planted little clumps of tussac, will slide helplessly through the ice towards the South Pole.

"On the way back," Alison says, as we set off again in the car, "we just need to put the girls through." I nod as though I know what this means, wondering who the girls are and what it is, exactly, they need putting through. (Their paces? Hell?) As we near a herd of cattle, it dawns on me that our task is to get eighteen pregnant cows through a gate into an area near the settlement.

Alison and I approach them, shouting and flapping our arms, and they look astonished and offended for a while and then veer away from us, usually in the wrong direction. I run to stop them, still flapping, trying to turn them around, and they shoot me glares that seem to say, *Well, you are just being impossible*, and then wander the right way for a while, before losing focus and meandering sideways. At one point, all eighteen of them are moving, together, towards the gate, their enormous bellies swaying under them. Then, instead of going through the opening, half of them walk right past it. When we try to reverse them they get skittish and scatter and we have to start again with the shouting and the flapping until, eventually, the last cow is through and the gate is shut.

I feel a huge sense of accomplishment when this is done. I consider trying to explain to Alison the pleasure of achieving something challenging and concrete and physically strenuous and patently useful. It's the opposite of writing, I would tell her, which leaves me mentally exhausted but physically unfit, which is rarely completed with any sense of certainty, and which is of unspecified and doubtful use to anyone. But in the end I don't say anything, and we drive on to the settlement in tired, satisfied silence.

Back in the house, I sit down to resume work on the book. I feel newly motivated, energized. I am so close to the end now. I have worked nearly all the way through the outline I made in my second week in Stanley, a neat diagram labelled with reassuring section headings: Situation, Complication, Climax, Resolution. It has continued to comfort and make sense to me long after the strange charts and graphs plotting *Bleaker House* against *Bleak House* have been discarded.

I have taken Ollie from his original situation through a series of complications according to this plan. Since coming up with it at the beginning of the trip, my day-to-day writing has been concerned not with what happens, but with how to express what I have already decided is going to happen. All I need to do, now I have reached the fourth and final sections of the narrative, is remind myself what I need to write next. I flick backwards through the pages of the notebooks, through sentences of description about the island interspersed with notes about word counts, weather, accidentally eating five more raisins than I was supposed to one day. I reach the plan. I find the following:

CLIMAX & RESOLUTION
Work this out! Everything comes together and all the questions are answered.

There is no other guidance. I close my laptop. I wander through the house, through the empty guest rooms where nobody else has stayed and then back to the sunroom, from where I can see the girls across the hillside. They are standing with their backs to the wind, heads bent to the ground, grazing and chewing and flicking their tails and looking as though they haven't been put through anything at all.

Fantasy Fiction

An idea arrives and you take it. Then, later, it takes you: to places, to people, and on this occasion to the basement Starbucks at Kenmore Square, where I am meeting a man who says his name is Chris. Later, he'll admit that this is not his real name.

This idea started as a dare. After Will, and Hong Kong, and Deptford, I left London and moved to Boston to study for my MFA in Fiction. I am ecstatic to be here: in America, writing, earning enough money through fellowships and teaching undergraduate classes to support myself. It is only when, at the end of my first semester, Leslie spreads out my first three stories in front of him on his desk and diagnoses me with "a failure of invention," that I begin to question myself again. I have produced a series of narratives about neurotic Londoners who worry about themselves and their lives and their health and their work. "A little more bravery," Leslie suggests.

My classmates and I get drunk in a bar near school and talk

about each other with a frankness normally reserved for the latter stages of a workshop. We brainstorm our weaknesses. We are brutal. I learn about my predictable endings, unconvincing female characters, prudish avoidance of sex scenes, and reliance on implausibly intellectual protagonists.

"You should write something different," someone says. "Write a character who, you know, isn't from London. Write a character with responsibilities—with a child."

"Write about a stripper," someone says. "Or a prostitute."

"Write about a stripper who becomes a prostitute."

And so, three weeks later I am sitting opposite Chris in Starbucks, pretending my name is Lisa and that I want to have sex with him for money.

I have trawled Craigslist for options. There are many. It is like learning a new language. Young, thin and willing? Contact me.—m4w—40 (Boston). Gentleman Benefactor Seeks . . . —34 (Boston). Schoolgirl? Young and Athletic? Discreet Daddy Here! (i can host today.)

The men are "benefactors" and "generous." They will "make donations' and "help with gas money." The ads are funny, and tragic, and disturbing, and specific: Toilet Time!!! Girlfriend into WWE? Looking for a girl with killer legs who loves sushi!

For most, I don't meet the criteria, and I suspect nobody does. Others are the ramblings of psychopaths. I scroll through Boston's sexual wish list seeking—What? A victim? A test subject? I am looking for a man who sounds unlikely to murder me, but unpleasant enough that I don't feel bad lying to him. I identify some possibilities and send off responses:

Hi! Just saw your ad on craigslist!
I am a twenty-seven-year-old grad student in Boston and

I would love to hear more about what you are looking for.
I'm originally from the UK, brunette, open-minded, and
looking for some extra cash.

Lisa x

Of the men who get back to me, Chris is the only one who
doesn't demand naked photos, so he's the one I pick.

In Starbucks, Chris says, "I thought this was a hoax."

When I lean my elbow on the edge of the table, trying to
look relaxed, it tilts towards me and his coffee splashes over the
surface.

He mops up the spill with napkins and goes on. "When I got
your email, I mean. I really thought it was a hoax. I didn't think
there'd be anyone here today."

He is in late middle age, and very short. The skin of his
cheeks has started to droop. The description he gave of himself
before we met—athletic build, full head of hair, blue eyes—is
not inaccurate, but still in no way resembles the man in front
of me. When I first noticed him, sitting in the corner of the
room looking around expectantly, drumming his fingers on the
blue book he said he'd be reading, my first thought was, *Please
let that not be him*. It's not that I was hoping to meet someone
attractive; it's just that he looks sad, more vulnerable, and also
somehow meaner than I expected. Perhaps, really, the problem
is that he looks, and is, real.

Before I have said a word, he reaches down and places a hand
firmly on my knee. A wedding band glints under the table.

"Hi," I say.

He leans his head in towards mine. His lips are very close to my ear. "I want to bend you over this table and fuck your brains out," he whispers.

It is ten in the morning and the cafe is full of college students bent over their laptops. I realize immediately that I should have picked a meeting place further from the university. I pull back a little and say, "Do you?" I try to smile in a way that both shuts the conversation down and suggests it could be opened again later.

Chris has a stay-at-home wife and cannot "host." He is looking for someone who can be extremely discreet, about two or three mornings a week. He loves my accent, he says, and he would be keen to start the "arrangement" as soon as possible. He wonders if I live nearby. I do, but tell him I don't, and he suggests we go for a drink instead. I make an elaborate show of googling bars in the vicinity, and try to act disappointed when I find that none are open yet. His grip on my knee never loosens.

"Let's wait until next time," I say.

We stand awkwardly out on the street saying goodbye. I am glancing around me, scared I'll be spotted by someone I know and anxious to get away. When I turn to leave, Chris grabs my wrist and leans in. I pull back but he still catches my lips with his and leaves wet saliva on my skin. I spend the rest of the day compulsively wiping my mouth.

When I next check the email account I have created for Lisa, there is already a message from Chris. It contains a story in which a character called Lisa does things to a character called Chris, and he does things to her, and the whole thing is so extravagant and far-fetched that it is more comic than erotic. It is like watching a puppet show operating at high speed. I don't reply.

Chris emails me laying out the details of his financial offer.

In return for two or three hours of my time and attention, he is willing to pay me two hundred dollars. I have no idea if this is a fair amount or not. I ask one of my MFA classmates and she tells me I should be offended.

Chris emails to check I got his last message, and to update me on how horny he is feeling. I don't reply.

Chris emails to express surprise that I haven't replied.

There are explosions at the finish line of the Boston Marathon. The news is full of pictures of the sidewalk wet with blood and the faces of people whose limbs have been blown off. That night, the bombers shoot a cop at MIT. One of the attackers is killed, the other gets away.

Chris emails to ask if I'm OK. Was I at the marathon? I don't reply.

A few days later, the whole city goes into lockdown and I spend the hours at home with a soundtrack of news, false news, recantations of false news, more news, and sirens. Police are searching basements for the missing bomber. Nobody is allowed to go outside. For a few minutes, I stand out on the back deck and listen to the sound of the dead city: a deep, unnatural silence. Through the windows of other houses, I can see the flicker of television screens. Then, from somewhere underneath me, there is a thud. A moment later: a series of scratches. The sounds are coming from the cellar, and I am briefly convinced that there is a terrorist hiding by the washing machine; then my neighbour emerges, carrying a basket of laundry.

To distract myself, I sit down to work on the story my classmates suggested, in which a stripper becomes a prostitute. I think of Chris, and feel sorry for him and disgusted by him and angry with him, and I try to write a character who is like him in some ways and not in others. I start the story over and over, and each time it doesn't ring true: I do not know if Chris is a good man or a bad man; I do not know if he is a victim or a predator; I do not know whether I am the one who should feel guilty.

In the evening, the newscasters announce that we are now allowed to leave our houses and it is as though someone has pressed play on a film. Everything begins to move. Traffic starts up on the high street nearby; people open their windows and music drifts out into the evening. This lasts for a few minutes and then we are all told to go back inside. The windows are slammed shut. Sirens wail. I check my messages.

Chris is upset. It's been a crazy week, he writes. So much has happened, and this whole time, he has been wondering about me. What's going on with me? That day in Starbucks, we had a connection, didn't we? There was a spark. When he touched my knee, he felt it, and he knows I felt it too—the way I kissed him on the street when we parted. How can I say, after everything that has happened, after everything we have shared, after feeling attraction the way we did—how can I say that I don't actually want to fuck him? Is this about the money?

I don't reply.

Three miles west of my apartment, on the other side of the river, the surviving bomber is discovered hiding in a boat in someone's back yard.

That evening everyone is restless. After a day spent cooped up inside, it feels daring and joyful to walk down the street. I meet friends in a bar, where the music is too loud for proper conversation, and instead we just smile and shout pointlessly and drink. The experience of being near each other, surrounded by people and movement and noise, is exhilarating.

My phone buzzes in my pocket, but instead of opening the new email, I remove Lisa's account. I never check it again.

I wonder whether Chris will keep writing to Lisa every day. I have accidentally, in my search for a character for my story, created a character who has invaded a real life. Perhaps Lisa will continue to exist for Chris, even after the idea for the story I wanted to write has faded in my mind. Or perhaps he will come to realize that she was never real, that he too had been writing a kind of story, had been searching for a character to use.

Despite himself, Ollie had imagined it would be warm inside the house. As the girl had led him towards the building, its corrugated-iron roof glowing slightly in the last of the moonlight, he had allowed himself to think that once they reached it, once they got inside, his situation would become bearable. Instead, when the door had shut out the weather and he had prised off his soaking boots, his shivering became so violent that at first he couldn't make out the words his companion was saying. The air around them was icy and still.

"What?" he said, through trembling lips. "What?"

The girl lit a match, and then a candle, which cast a halo of light on their surroundings. They were in a kitchen, with a small, uneven-looking table in the middle of the room and an empty tin bath occupying one corner. She moved around, lighting more candles until the space was so bright it gave the faintest suggestion of heat, and Ollie's breathing began to return to normal. She gestured to him to take a seat.

"I said, this is Bleaker House."

Apart from the wind whistling through cracks in the windowpanes and the gap under the door, the place was silent. Ollie sat at the table, which wobbled as he leaned his elbows on it, and surveyed the room: a grease-slimed stove, the rusting bath, overwhelming clutter. Crumbs, cutlery, cooking utensils, and scraps of food were spread out on the counters, the stove, the tabletop, and the floor. A half-plucked bird, its eyes glazed, lay in a pile of its own feathers on a counter. There was no sign of any electricity, no gas; it was as though he had stepped back in time—as though the plane had dropped him off, all those hours earlier, in a different century.

The things the girl had told him on the walk to the house— casually, as though she were recapping rather than revealing anything—seemed unreal, still. He realized he was tense, sitting on the edge of his seat, braced for a punchline that had yet to come.

"He's really here?" he said, eventually. "My father—you mean he really is alive?"

The girl nodded and sighed, seeming irritated by the question. "You knew that before you got here, Oliver, otherwise you never would have bothered to make the journey."

"And you—you really are my sister? You've been here all along?"

"Were you not listening when I told you before?"

In his defence, Ollie thought, it had been hard to hear, as they had stomped through the mud, following the trembling dot of the girl's torch, and she had told him as though it were a reasonable situation that her name was Cressida; that she was his half-sister; that she had been six months old when Alsop, their father, had left to make his fortune in England; that after the humiliation of his accident at the hands of the toaster he had returned in secret to the Falklands and lived out his life as a recluse on Bleaker Island. Over the combined roar of waves hitting the cliffs and wind punching in from the ocean, her voice had seemed faint and unconvincing.

"And you really have lived here with him in secret all this time?"

She shrugged. "Evidently. Well, when Mummy was alive she was here too, obviously. She and I arranged for everything—for food and fuel and animal feed and such—with help from a few people on the other islands who agreed not to ask too many questions. Sometimes I take the boat across to the mainland and sneak into Stanley—I'm good at not being noticed—to use the Internet and things like that. That's how I found out about you, in fact—I found your picture and I just knew you were Daddy's son. Of course Daddy didn't want anyone to know we were here. He loved being dead. But now he really is dying, Oliver, and I want him to see you. You took your sweet time getting here—it could have been too late, you know."

"So he knows who I am?" Ollie asked. "I mean, he knows I exist?"

For the first time, Cressida paused and seemed to give his question thought. She sat down opposite him and planted her elbows so forcefully on the table that the piles of crockery that covered it clattered and shifted. She opened her mouth to answer, and then closed it again. In the candlelight, her whole face seemed unearthly. Blue veins shone from her temples. Ollie had the impression of sitting down to talk with a ghost.

"I've told him."

"He knows I'm here?"

She gave a slight nod. "He will have heard the plane arriving, same as I did."

"And how come it was you who wrote the letter, and not him?"

She bit her lip and fixed her eyes on Ollie's hands. With her gaze averted, he took the chance to study her again. He considered her pale brittleness and the way her life story—this secret existence on an island in the middle of an angry, wide ocean—seemed writ large on her body. She looked not quite human, he thought. She looked like a different species.

"I think he's embarrassed, Oliver."

"Embarrassed of what?"

Cressida stood, abruptly. "It's late. You should get some sleep. I'll take you to him in the morning."

She picked up a candle and handed another to Ollie. He followed her out of the kitchen, down a narrow corridor, and into a small, empty room with a mattress on the floor. "Will this be OK? I'll bring you blankets."

Ollie watched the flickering of her light grow dimmer down the corridor, then dropped his bag on the floor and placed his candle in one corner of the room. The mattress was lumpy, and when he got close to it he saw it was made of sacking sewn together over some kind of dry grass. When he sat down, it made a loud crunch.

"Here." Cressida was in the doorway. She dropped some heavy, woollen blankets at his feet.

"Thanks."

"Goodnight."

"Goodnight."

She was lingering still. The light was too dim to make out

her expression. Ollie wondered whether he was expected to say something else, whether he had disappointed her in some way.

"He thinks," she said, after a while, "that if you've come half-way around the world to find him, he has to be good enough. He sets great store by the idea of being . . . manly. Strong."

A phrase, "the fracturing of the patriarchal ideal," appeared in Ollie's mind, and it took him a moment to recognize it as a chapter heading from his own thesis. The thought was jarring, like a recovered memory from a previous life. "I see," he said. He knew nothing about masculinity. What had he written in his thesis? What had all those words amounted to? He knew nothing about being manly.

Cressida walked away.

Ollie woke disoriented and so cold he couldn't move. Rigid on the mattress, he put together the events of the previous day, recalling the strange and unlikely information Cressida had relayed to him, and finally realizing, almost for the first time, that he had made it—that he was really there, on Bleaker Island. He was about to meet a person who for the majority of his life had not existed, and who, since he first left Oxford for the Falklands, had seemed like an embarrassing fantasy rather than a plausible destination.

He was about to meet his father.

After several failed attempts, he managed to sit up, and then stand. He walked shakily to the window and regarded the island in the dawn light. He had seen some of it from the plane, and for thirty minutes or so after landing before the sun had set, but now, the view from the house was startling. He was looking out over a bay filled with dark, rough water that was pummel-ling the shore so violently it made him sway. Overhead, clouds pressed down as though hoping to crush the island back into the water. Ollie leaned against the glass.

He was about to meet his father.

More than nerves, more than excitement, more than anything, what he felt now was satisfaction. He was about to be vindicated. This long journey—its indignities and ridiculousness and doubt, loneliness, hardship—was about to be proved worthwhile. His instincts and curiosity had led him, eventually, to the right place, and now he would collect his reward. He felt, then, at the window, trying to curl and straighten his numb fingers against the glass, that it almost didn't matter who his father was or what he was like. The point was that his father existed, was alive, and that he, Ollie, had tracked him down. The point was that he would go home having gained something real.

Somewhere behind him in the house, footsteps were shuffling and thudding. A door slammed. Ollie turned and took a step across the mattress towards it when he heard Cressida's voice.

"Oliver?" she was calling. "Oliver!"

He trotted out of the room, down the corridor, and into the kitchen, where his sister was standing barefoot on the floor, glancing about her as though she were hallucinating. She was clutching her white-blond hair so tightly he thought it would come out in her fists.

"Oliver," she said breathily, when she saw him. "You have to help me."

"What? What's happened?"

"It's Daddy," she said. "He's not here. I can't find him. He's gone."

Lost Plot, Long Gulch

am ashamed of my book. My book is no good. I am ashamed of myself for writing this bad book.

My final days on Bleaker Island are full of snowstorms. Amid flurries and blizzards and sleet, I write and delete paragraphs over and over. I am restless and dissatisfied with myself. The resolution of the novel—the point up to which everything I have written so far has been building—eludes me. I have brought Ollie from Oxford to the Falklands; I have led him on a dance all around Stanley and finally got him to Bleaker; and now that he is here, he should be confronting the person who makes his journey worthwhile—his and the reader's, too—and I can't find a way to write it.

I am trying to keep certain thoughts at bay, in particular the horrifying, devastating idea that this thing I have been writing, all the thousands and thousands and thousands of words of it, is a failure. Not only will I not finish it before I leave the island, but maybe I won't finish it at all, ever. I find myself shaking my head a lot, as though I could dislodge this fear from my brain the way the sheep outside twitch snow off their backs. It doesn't work, though—not for me, and not, ultimately, for the sheep either, who wander around with saddles of compacted snow, getting stuck in deep drifts. George tells me that they suffocate if he can't pull them out in time. They get disorientated. They stumble off the edges of cliffs.

If the novel is a failure, if I truly cannot write it, then all this has been for nothing. I have been sitting alone on a small snowy island for weeks and weeks—for nothing. I have been hungry and alone and cold—for nothing.

Through the window and the curtain of weather, I see George setting off across the hills in his jeep, searching for lost livestock, hoping to drag them out of the ditches before it's too late.

In four days' time, I will be leaving Bleaker. There are four Ferrero Rochers left in the final box, four granola bars, and now, four apples in their neat line in the kitchen. I have anticipated my departure with such fervour for so long now that I can't bear to look at the date on the itinerary. All that excitement I had about leaving was not just because it meant a return to food, and different clothes, and company; it was because by then I thought I'd have a completed novel that would validate everything I'd put myself through. I knew it would be a rough draft, and that I would need to work on it and rewrite it and adjust it when I got home. But it never once crossed my mind that what I would produce on the island would be *bad*, or somehow un-finish-able. Now, in these final days, I find myself in the unnerving position of wanting to stay longer, because the thought of more isolation and hunger and chill is not nearly as appalling as the thought of going home with nothing to show for my time here.

I have been foolish. How could I have thought that sitting down to write a set number of words each day was the recipe for good writing? Of course it doesn't work like that. Amassing thousands of words together in a single Word document is no achievement at all if the words are poorly chosen, or in the wrong order, or both. How did I expect to write well with nobody to discuss it with, and while my stomach was crying out constantly for solid food?

I make a pilgrimage to the kitchen to visit the potato. If there ever was a time for it, I think, it's now. Except that now, when I need it most, I feel I least deserve it. The potato would feel like a celebration of my failure, and I refuse to celebrate my failure.

What is the problem with the novel? I stare at the screen and the words on the white pages. It is as though a spell has been broken. There were days—I know there were, I remember them—when the words came easily. I was convinced by the story I was telling, by Ollie himself and the world in which I had placed him. I believed in him. There were those times when I was so caught up in what I'd written that I would feel nervous, as though I were being watched, and I'd close the curtains because it felt possible that things could come to life, that having written what I'd written, I was no longer really alone.

Now, it feels as though I have woken from a dream. Ollie is not real. He is, in fact, a silly character—flat, caricatured, clownish. He is always falling over, I realize. He is always doing things that make him blush. The reader is in a constant state of feeling smarter than him, of knowing more about his life and situation than he does. What was it Leslie told us? *It is particularly unbecoming for a young person to look down his nose at his characters—too easy, too slack, a stance that has almost certainly not been earned through one's experience of life.*

The plot calls on me now to deliver a long-lost father to Ollie. My protagonist has travelled halfway around the world on a quest that I myself established for him, and it is now my responsibility to resolve it, and I can't. The scenarios I come up with become increasingly ludicrous. It strikes me as no coincidence that, when it comes down to it, Ollie's father is running away from him: I do not know how to write a convincing reconciliation.

In a moment of grim, self-hating anti-humour I delete three attempts at paragraphs and write in their place, "And he woke up and it was all a dream," even though it is me, and not Ollie, who has woken up.

I have not left the house since the storms began three days ago, and this, paired with a longer-than-usual Internet failure, is surely contributing to my increasing anguish. It's still snowing outside, and the wind is shrieking, but going out seems more inviting than staying at home with my anxieties. I put on almost every item of clothing I have, including two hats and an extra scarf wrapped around my waist as a kind of girdle, and step outside. The flat force of the wind hits me like a slap.

There is a place called Long Gulch that I've seen on the map of the island hanging in the sunroom. It is a long thin crack in the side of the island, as though the rock has begun to split, and in all my wanderings I've never seen it. I have it in my mind to get there now—a vague sense that it is not far from the settlement and that reaching it will therefore be a quick, neat excursion, long enough to distract me from my worries, not so long that I will catch hypothermia.

I stagger along my normal route towards the beach, then south along the coast, bending sideways into the gale. The sky is filled with so many birds that they look like a new kind of weather: seagulls emerging from waves like an extension of the spray, grey wings overhead dripping down from the clouds.

Something large and black flies past and dives into the ground behind me. I assume it is the caracara again, but when I look back I realize it's a hooded sweatshirt of mine, emblazoned with the letters "BU," mud-soaked and now plastered flat against a tuft of tussac. I washed it days ago, hung it up outside with the rest of my laundry and somehow didn't notice it had blown away when I brought the other things in. I suppose it has been on a frenzied journey ever since, whirling around the island, dipping into bogs and up again. I dither about whether or not to pick it up, then, when I inspect it more closely, see that it is covered in cow dung; I leave it where it is. I set off again, wondering what else I have lost here, whether there are odd socks swimming alongside the swans in Big Pond, bras setting sail towards Antarctica.

Up ahead: Long Gulch. Before I see the crevice itself, I notice plumes of water rising up where it looks as though there should be solid land. It snows and hails in fits and starts, stinging. I pull the cord of my hood tight around my face so I have only a small tunnel to see out of. My feet are sliding around on the mud as though I'm learning how to skate. When I get to the gulch, my muscles are burning, the skin around my lips is stinging in the cold, and the waves are raging.

I stumble down into a small cranny out of the wind and

crouch there, panting, to watch the ocean. The waves are wild, smashing against the rocks and sending up walls of spray. The whole gully is filled with thick, foamy water that looks like churning whipped cream. It oozes and folds back on itself, sucking kelp under its surface, then spitting it back up. I am transfixed. I barely notice the gradual loss of sensation in my feet and hands. There is a comforting fascination in witnessing from nearby something that could kill you in a second: the black water turning white as it hurls itself against the rocks.

As I stare at the water and boulders and the birds that, thanks to Alison, I now know are night herons nestling in the nooks, I have an unsettling idea about the novel, and in a strange way about *Bleak House,* too—something so huge it makes my stomach clench—and before I know it, I have stood up into the blast of the wind, and am scrambling to get back home. My feet are numb and I'm walking oddly, tripping over my own boots. I need to think about this huge, bizarre, alarming thing in peace, away from the waves.

I try to focus on my location for a moment, plotting out a map of the route I've traced in my head: I have walked two sides of a triangle to get to Long Gulch, so if I head away from the coast across the thin central strip of the island I will complete the third. This is the quickest, most direct route. I'm freezing and tired, but it should only take twenty minutes to get back, I tell myself. Before I know it I'll be warm again, and sitting in front of my laptop in the sunroom. I'm nearly home. I'm nearly home. The wind is pounding my back as though it too wants me to hurry, is pushing me onwards. I stride and slither over mud.

When I reach the place where I expect the house to be, I find instead a sheer cliff. The ground stops suddenly, and beneath is a long, abrupt drop into dark water. I was so certain of my route, but here, where I thought I'd find not only solid ground, but the comfort of the house, dry clothes and my book, there is only thin air.

I back away from the edge. The sun is sinking, and it is beginning to snow hard again and what I thought were the sheep that habitually graze near the settlement reveal themselves to be, now, nothing but white patches of ice-coated tussac. I do not know where I am, I think. I don't know how to get back to the house, I think. More than anything, I think how incredibly embarrassing it is to get lost on an island this small.

I know there are cliffs on only one of the coasts; I know the wind was against me when I left and is now at my back; I know I can be at most two miles from the house and that I should be able to navigate from the position of the sun if nothing else, but somehow I can't see anything familiar, and the snow makes everything look different anyway. A fog is descending that cuts off my vision after a few feet. I wander in circles, recalling those passages from the *Falkland Islands Magazine* reporting local deaths in the nineteenth century. It seemed so ludicrous, when I first read those articles, that so many people would get stuck in bogs and wander off cliffs and get lost, alone, on small islands. Now, I compose an article about myself: "Foolhardy Writer Loses Way, Is Pecked to Death by Caracaras."

Then, suddenly, the wind changes. Instead of pelting snow at the back of my head, it now pummels the side of my face, and carries with it the pungent, unmistakable odour of penguins.

I don't think I've ever been, or ever will be, more delighted by the smell of rotting fish. I rush towards it, praying it won't change direction again, following the scent. Eventually, over the crest of the hill, the colony of gentoos appears, nestled at the far end of the white curve of the beach. From here it is only a thirty-minute walk home, on my usual path, and by the time I get back it has stopped snowing for the first time in days. I watch the last of the sun vanish into water that looks oddly calm.

Here's the thought that struck me at Long Gulch: I could sort out Ollie's character; I could make him more rounded, less goofy and introspective. I could change the language, too—go back and write it in first or even second person, switch up the tense, adopt a cleaner style. I could prune out all those contorted, grammatically distorting, seemingly never-ending sentences. I could do all that, but there would still be a problem, something unfixable, and that is the original premise, which will never, ever be believable. It is a fairy tale asking to be taken at face value. There is no way that a character like Ollie, being who he is, would ever end up in a place like Bleaker in search of his father. It would never happen. It is too far, and too random, and too ridiculous, and too strange. He wouldn't even make it to Stanley.

The only person who would end up on Bleaker Island, I think, is me. The only reason anyone would come here alone, and stay for so long with nothing to do, is to write about it.

I scroll upwards through pages and pages of the novel, then turn back through the notebooks. My mind is still full of the swirling chaos at Long Gulch, and instead of my unfathomable *Bleak House* charts, what catches my eye now are the scribbled diary entries that appear between attempts to draw Ollie's family tree: the daily attempts I made to write, by hand, about the island. There are pages and pages and pages of these notes.

· Monday 2nd September: Snow has come back to the mainland; white hillsides creased like bed sheets. Sun sinking
into it.

· Saturday 24th August: Wide, wide sky tonight, still glowing
where the light was, that luminous blue, orange at the edge,
faint stars and a large one, brighter than the others. Found a
can of tinned pears in the cupboard and tried melting a Ferrero Rocher onto the fruit in the microwave. Ruined both
chocolate and pear so will not repeat.

· Wednesday 7th August: Today my eyes are heavy and tight,
and I'm listless, and suddenly so frustrated to find myself on
a small island, surrounded by snow, cut off from all of the rest
of life. I got up and did my exercises just the same, and sat in
the sunroom and stared at the patch of world outside—snow,
geese, red-roofed sheds—and imagined all the things I want
to do next, all the places I want to go: London; New York;
increasingly, passionately, Rome. Perhaps this. Perhaps that.
Plans plans plans. But then I look up and I find I am still on a
cold island in the South Atlantic.

Next, I turn to *Bleak House*, which has sat like a talisman beside
my laptop all this time. I skim the pages of Esther's narrative,
noticing in a way I never have before the persistence of the
personal pronoun: "I," says Esther. "I, I, I. I thought. I felt. I
wished."

Bleak House isn't only court cases, scrap paper, the search for
lost family. It is also about the awkward surrealness of attempting to narrate one's own life. Somehow, until now, I didn't see
that.

"It seems so curious to me to be obliged to write all this
about myself!" says Esther. "As if this narrative were the narra-

tive of MY life!" But so much of *Bleak House* is the narrative of her life. Even when she doesn't know it, the story she is telling is her own.

What if the book I thought I was writing is not the book that I have really written? What if I have spent my time on the island thinking I was writing about Ollie, while accidentally, almost incidentally, between the pages if not between the lines, I have been putting together a different book altogether? What if the story of *Bleaker House* is the narrative of MY life?

When the snow begins to melt, giant petrels circle and descend on the carcases of sheep lost in the storm. They feast on the corpses until there is nothing left but fleece and bones, and they are too bloated and heavy to fly. I watch them struggling on the ground, hopping and flapping hopelessly, lurching over rocks as they try and fail to take off.

Bleaker House: RESOLUTION

Loneliness Is a City You Don't Know

This is not a voyage of self-discovery. This is not a healing process. This is not one woman's search for everything, or a journey from lost to found.

I did not come to Bleaker Island to find myself.

I came here to work—to write a book.

Except didn't I also, really, come for those other things? To learn how to be alone? To discover the authentic core of myself? The idea of this makes me cringe. But what should I think of myself, now, as the end of my exile on Bleaker arrives and I have not done what I ostensibly set out to do? There is no finished novel. Instead there is this strange, surprising, amorphous thing, this other kind of story I have accidentally, fragmentarily, told. I feel as though I have pulled a rabbit from a hat I was about to put on.

I think back to my fellowship proposal, that optimistic pitch about concentration and solitude. There was so much more I wanted to accomplish here than the one thing I have failed, it transpires, to do. I was scared of being alone. I was scared that I would always be alone. I was scared that this fear, this boring, ordinary fear of loneliness, would obstruct my writing by making me weak. And so, I thought, if I could handle all this time by myself on Bleaker Island, it would mean I could handle being alone in real life. It was supposed to be a kind of home-made immersion therapy.

After Will, I went out with a poet who, on a Friday night, took me to a poetry reading in Farringdon, across the road from a strip club. After drinking to the point of silliness at the reading, we staggered across to the club and spent the rest of the night with the strippers.

"Get a dance," the poet said. "Get a dance from one of the girls."

I had come out straight from work. I was wearing a light grey woollen dress and tights. This seemed acceptable attire for a poetry reading, but next to the semi-naked woman crawling across the table towards me, I felt laughable. She looked awkward, too, but tried to do her job as best she could, while I attempted to make small talk. "Where do you come from? How long have you worked here for? Do you like your job?"

She stopped writhing. "Do you want me to tell you stories, or do you want me to dance?"

The poet and I didn't see each other again after that night.

A year or so later, I googled him and ordered a copy of his book. It arrived: a shiny black cover, his name in bold letters that made it look distant and unfamiliar. I flicked through the contents until I reached a poem that made me pause. I read and re-read the first line: "Not every love leaves. Some tarry, ever visceral; every nerve singing." I stared. Then I saw it. The first letter of each word lined up: "N E L L S T E V E N S."

I felt uncomfortable, exposed, as though something had been taken from me without my permission. It was not true, what he had written. Our love definitely left. He could have got the same effect with "Not every love lasts." He didn't have to lie about it.

Reading something that has been written about you is like looking into a mirror and seeing another person's face.

All along, you thought those people understood who you really are, and it turns out they were seeing someone else entirely.

In Boston, I was invited to a dinner party in the middle of a snowstorm. The host was a woman in my fiction workshop. The city had shut down in the blizzard and the woman lived across town. I was at home, curled up on my bed in tracksuit bottoms and slippers, reading and watching snow gradually blot out the view through my windowpane. It was warm inside. I was drowsy and comfortable. I began to craft a delicate negative response to the invite, citing the weather along with a deadline I had for a story the coming week, but before I had time to send it, she texted, "OK, well, forget it," and somehow, in a rush to appease her, I ended up replying that of course I'd be there, would love to be there, would bring wine and arrive for eight.

I spent thirty minutes shuffling around my neighbourhood in the storm, looking for a cab willing to make the trip, and eventually reached her apartment nearly an hour late. I walked in full of apologies, expecting dinner to be under way, to be squeezed in at the end of a table of busily eating, laughing guests. But nobody else was there. The room was silent. The woman had laid the table for two.

"Nobody else could make it," she said.

We ate sitting opposite each other, and drank her bottle of

wine, and then the one that I had brought, and then whisky. At some point after dinner, she suggested we go snowshoeing, and with only one pair between us, this meant waddling about, falling over a lot, picking each other up, holding hands. Around two, I told her I should get a cab. She shrugged. When I called the taxi companies, I found that none of them was operating because of the blizzard.

"So, you'll have to stay," the woman said. She reached across, moved hair back from my face and leaned in to kiss me.

I should not have stayed, of course—because the weather was no better the next morning and I still had to walk across the city in snow that was, at times, waist-high; because I then spent the rest of the academic year screening her calls and trying to avoid her because I didn't know how to explain why I did stay that night; and because in our final workshop she submitted a story in which an insecure, unknown artist has a passionate one-night stand with a successful painter, then flees and never answers his calls because she fears she doesn't deserve the happiness that a relationship with him would inevitably bring. The woman read excerpts aloud to the group, fixing her eyes on me over the top of the paper.

I was, again, indignant. Her portrayal was inaccurate. It was self-aggrandizing and unfair. I was full of remonstrance—I suddenly wanted to speak to this person I had been studiously avoiding, just to say, *The reason I have been studiously avoiding you is not because I am uncomfortable with happiness, or with my sexuality, but because I am uncomfortable around you*. I didn't say anything. Instead, I resolved to take the high ground and never, ever write about her.

Months later, her story came out in a magazine. The title had changed, and the couple got together at the end, which is what Leslie had suggested in class.

. . .

It seems clear, now, that I have been alone in my relationships. When people I have dated write about me, I see it that way. When I write about them, they must see, too, that I was not there with them, but with some other person, a kind of shallow twin of theirs. It is hard to love someone, if you are in the habit of taking every experience you have as material for your work. It has surely been doubly hard when both partners are in it for the same thing: a kind of mutual excavation, digging rather than caring.

Is the life of a writer necessarily a lonely one? Part of my decision to come to Bleaker Island came from a place of pessimism: I feared that this was the case. I have been in training for loneliness.

The problem with this idea, though, is that, as I turn through the pages and pages of diary entries, it does not seem to me that I have been truly lonely on the island. I have been a lot of other things—bored, hungry, frustrated, and lately, disappointed in myself—but not really, specifically lonely.

It occurs to me that if you want to be completely alone, the place to go would be a city you don't know. On Bleaker, where company is scarce, my own has become by comparison quite fascinating. I have been on excellent speaking terms with myself, happily narrating my thoughts and days as I stride up to the beach, or around the pond, arguing points, and asking myself questions. I don't even notice I'm doing it until another sound—a birdcall or a particularly loud gust of wind—draws my attention away from my own voice. I have been working my way through the CDs sent by my novelist friend, and sometimes, when an unexpected track comes on, it makes me look up from whatever I am doing, and it feels as though he is suddenly in the room with me, smiling and saying, "Yes, what about this?" When George and Alison returned from their time away and resumed their daily mid-morning visits, the company felt almost overwhelming.

In Hong Kong, I understand now, I was lonely. When I moved to Boston for the very first time and knew nobody, I would go on long, solitary walks by the Charles past couples arm in arm and groups of teenagers smoking on the benches; then, I was lonely. Sometimes in London, too, when my friends were away and I hadn't seen anyone for a few days, I'd sit on the 68 bus going over Waterloo Bridge and feel the ache developing. Surrounded by people, it is very easy to feel alone. Surrounded by penguins, less so.

For a few weeks, I dated a composer. After we broke up, he set some of my writing to music. I went to see it performed by a Dutch baritone and Spanish guitar at Wigmore Hall. It was an atonal, arrhythmic blur of sound, and I didn't know enough about new music to work out whether or not I should be offended.

On my final night on Bleaker, I go walking at dusk in the last of the light. Snow on the mainland makes the curves and dips of small hills on the horizon look like a distant mountain range: the beginning of the wide other world that I will soon return to.

On the beach, the colony of penguins is growing. They appear in the water, diving in arcs through the waves in groups of three or four, then reach the sand and waddle, wings outstretched, to join the waiting cluster. Spring is coming. They are gathering to breed.

On the other side of the island, the sun is drooping and then gone from sight. Suddenly the wind dies, and stays dead. It is strange, the silence now, with only the birdcalls to break it. The water is still and silvery, paler than the sky, as though it remembers the light that has faded.

I look around: there is no movement except for the swerving of birds. A neat V-formation slides above the water. Back at the settlement, George and Alison will be at home, cooking, talking to each other, living their normal life. Tomorrow, I will have left the island and they will remain. Nothing will have changed for them at all.

For now, though, the place stills feels as though it is mine. Nobody is here. Nobody can see me. And what that makes me want to do is—dance.

I am ridiculous, twirling and swooping and jumping between little mounds of grass that poke up from the snow, the way I would have done when I was little. I laugh at myself, and then feel very serious, and leap as high as I possibly can in the air.

I am alone, and can do anything. I am alone and not lonely. I have come to the end of my time on the island without writing what I set out to write, with an unfinished failure of a novel, a mass of incoherent diary entries and only the vaguest sense of what to do with them; and yet I feel, more now than ever before, that I am a writer. I land with a thud, sending mud and guano flying.

"Character Study"

You knew him as a man first, and a character in a poetry book second. You had seen him at the school gates, waiting for Mrs. Grant, your English teacher. Sometimes you even acknowledged him. You said, "Hello, Mr. Grant," in a voice you knew—you had studied and perfected it—combined insolence and politeness in perfect balance, so that he was flummoxed, unsure whether to be angry, or embarrassed, or to return the greeting in good faith. You trailed your fingers along the school railings and stalked off. You imagined his gaze following you down the road—but when you swung around with a gasp and "Gotcha" eyes, he was looking the other way.

It wasn't you who found the poems. It was a girl in your class called Victoria Collins, who ran into the classroom and slowed to a knowing swagger before dropping the book on the desk in front of everyone. The hands of the clock were edging towards eight-thirty, when your form tutor would appear to take the register.

"What is that?" you asked. You often spoke like this, on behalf of the group. People allowed you to.

Victoria paused for effect and the room, which had been filled with drowsy early-morning chatter and the shuffle of books and homework being unpacked, was quiet. "Mrs. Grant," she said. She stopped. Then, "Mrs. Grant is a poet. I found her book in the library."

There was an air of immediate disappointment. Victoria had oversold the news; it was nothing interesting. Your social worlds already included poets. Your parents and their friends, academics at the university for the most part, or publishing people at the university press, had made poets commonplace to you all. You had suffered through dinner parties with poets. Poets had bored you.

The news was, at best, vaguely embarrassing for Mrs. Grant. It was awkward for her that she had been found out this way. If she had wanted her students to know about the book, she would have told you herself. There was an additional though minor thrill in discovering the thing your teachers had wanted to be before they became teachers; a badge of failure suddenly unveiled.

But you felt it was a defeat for you personally, too, since you hadn't known about it until now, and the book had been sitting in the library all along. This was the sort of thing you usually made it your business to discover. You turned your back and began rummaging in your rucksack for chewing gum.

Victoria knew she was losing the crowd. She had clearly expected more interest. "Sex poems," she blurted out. "The book. It's full of poems about her and Mr. Grant having sex."

You looked up, and smiled, and Victoria's face flushed. A triumph.

"Give that to me," you said. She slid the book across the desk to your waiting hand.

You read it that afternoon after school, sitting on top of a line of garages at the end of your road. You could climb up via a low wall and a tree, and smoke undisturbed. People passing by on the pavement below had no idea you were there; when you were younger you had entertained yourself by throwing flecks of gravel down at them and watching their bemused faces turn to look up at the sky. Now, you preferred to keep an absolute distance from the rest of the world.

You kept a box of private things tucked behind the drainpipe, things you didn't want your mother to find when she searched your room: condoms; a little bag of weed you bought from someone's older brother; a razor blade you had confiscated from a girl at school called Natalie Price, who was always threatening to kill herself. There were some pills you had ordered from the back of a magazine that promised to dissolve your fat, and torn-out, glossy articles listing tips for giving blow jobs, or getting a beach body in two weeks. These were the kinds of secrets you expected yourself to have. Mrs. Grant's poetry book was different and surprising to you, because you wanted it for yourself, and it felt too private even for the drainpipe box.

Its cover was an expanse of blank, dark blue, interrupted in the bottom-left corner by a honeycomb pattern of hexagons in pink. The title and her name were spelled in white letters: *Tessellations,* by Bethany Grant.

At first you skimmed the pages for the sex bits. You found

lines about Mr. Grant's penis, about rippling orgasms, about sweat and semen and screams, and a list of "love items" that included his "cut-out buttocks, rising like dust up beyond the window." None of it rhymed, which was a relief. You had studied Sylvia Plath in Mrs. Grant's class that year and understood that poems could either rhyme, or be interesting, but never both. "We two, heat-hunched and folded so we fell," the verse continued, "stripped pink like worms in dirt."

Tessellations was not disappointing, even when you reached the last page. Then you went back, reading more slowly, filling in the bits between the sex scenes; there was a narrative to it, you discovered, about the two of them meeting, the relationship developing, Mr. Grant playing love songs on his piano, then the vitiligo that spread across his skin like clouds and the wedding that took place on the anniversary of the death of his twin brother. You were good at English, good at reading and understanding and imagining things; when you reached the end a second time, you found that you still weren't finished with it, and started all over again. "Piano goes and goes and I love you," it said, on the final page, "over-exposed in front of the sun, and so—whiter in parts than even you are."

It was late, and you were hungry. The smells of other people's evening meals drifted from the nearby houses up to the garage roofs: roast chicken, garlic. You shuffled backwards down from the ledge, scuffing the leather of your shoes against the bark of the tree and landing with a thud that jolted your knees.

At dinner, your mother and father sat and talked civilly, and you realized for the first time that they didn't dislike each other as much as you used to think; they just weren't in love the way Mr. and Mrs. Grant were in love.

. . .

Mrs. Grant taught a class about control and mastery in *The Tempest*. She talked about the power of language, about Caliban and Prospero and the relationship between emotion and the ability to articulate emotion. As she spoke, you scrutinized her. It was hard to tell how old she was—younger than most of the other teachers, certainly, but ages blurred into each other once you got past twenty or so. They looked like adults to you, and all the same.

It occurred to you for the first time that Mrs. Grant might be pretty. She had dark black hair that she flipped from one side of her head to the other when she spoke; she wore the kinds of shoes you yourself imagined you would wear when you were older. You tried to picture her taking off her clothes. You thought about the naked body underneath them: a real woman's body that was unlike yours or your friends', but also unlike your mother's or the crumpled, pillowy shapes of the women in the locker room at the swimming pool. You tried to hear the way her voice would soften when she was with Mr. Grant, see the expression on her face when he was playing music for her, or when she was admiring his cut-out buttocks. You had never felt jealous of a teacher before, but this sudden vision of a whole world occupied by Mrs. Grant outside the classroom was shocking, and wonderful. She snapped her fingers in front of you.

"Hey, Emma, Daydreamer, I asked you a question," she said.

"I don't know," you said. You were careful to give your voice no inflection, your face no expression.

Because you were bored by school, and by your best friend, Caroline, and by the week, which was the last of the academic year. Because soon the summer holidays would begin and the prospect, which normally seemed so full of opportunity, now struck you as unbearably empty and sad. Because the way you felt when you were reading *Tessellations,* the concentration, breathlessness, the heat between your legs, was a form of joy and not boring. Because you were curious. Because it would be scandalous. Because you, too, would be scandalized if you actually went through with it.

Because Mrs. Grant's poems made something happen in your mind—made you feel both identified and unfamiliar, made you feel hungry. Because you understood, suddenly, that there were people all around you living different kinds of lives, and Mrs. Grant's was only one of them, and truly you wanted more than that, you wanted to learn and feel all sorts of other things, but you had to start somewhere. Because you were sick of being yourself, of being sixteen, of not being touched by anyone but boys from the boys' school, who always told everyone everything afterwards and got cum in your hair, or on your clothes.

Mr. Grant wasn't waiting at the gate that day, or the next day, which was the end of term. You looked him up in the phone book. You didn't really know what you wanted. You thought you'd just call the number to check it was the right Grant.

Answering machine: *Liam and Bethany, leave a message after the beep.* You weren't planning on saying anything, but when the moment came, you blurted out a line from one of the poems in *Tessellations* and then hung up, heart thudding.

Five minutes later, the house phone rang, and you had already forgotten about the call you'd made. You answered as you normally would, hoping it would be one of your friends. When you heard a man's voice on the end of the line, you assumed it was someone for your parents.

"Did you just call this number?" he said. "I got a weird message on the answering machine—something about a dark park?"

"It's from one of her poems," you said.

"Who is this?"

You did not want to lie. "Emma James."

"Who?"

"From school." You often lied, but sensed that doing so now would take the giddy joy out of what was happening.

"So," he sounded baffled, but pressed on, "you wanted to speak to Bethany?"

In the spirit of this new adrenalin-fuelled honesty, you were about to say "No," but he continued to speak.

"You're out of luck," he said. "She's away for the whole summer on her fellowship. She left this morning."

"What fellowship?"

"The writing fellowship. She left today. Didn't she tell—haven't you—wait, who is this?"

"Emma James," you said again.

He exhaled so loudly the receiver crackled. "I assumed you were a friend of Beth's from work."

"No," you said. "I'm not her friend. I didn't know about the fellowship."

He sighed again, and you thought you could hear his tongue moving through spit in his mouth. You wondered what you should say next—whether you should ask him about his vitiligo, or his dead twin, or apologize for everything. Before you made up your mind, he hung up.

You were ashamed of the phone call. You knew it had been odd behaviour, and you didn't like to think, now, of Mrs. Grant hearing about it. Perhaps, though, since she was away, he wouldn't remember to tell her. Perhaps by the time she got back he'd have forgotten it happened, or at least forgotten your name.

You told Caroline about it, making it sound as funny as possible. He was a heavy breather, you said. He asked what you were wearing. He asked you to go round there and keep him company while Mrs. Grant was away on her fellowship. He was touching himself while you were speaking, you could tell. She gasped and laughed and asked if you really would do it—go round there—and you said you would and she said you were crazy, but crazy in a fun way, not crazy like Natalie Price.

He answered the door in his pyjamas, which took you aback, because it was only six p.m., and a Tuesday. He looked different from how he did at the school gates, when he had always seemed so neat, clean-shaven, wearing chinos and button-down shirts. Now, he had a dark shadow of stubble across his cheeks and chin, and bare feet. You peered at them, scanning for the pale blotches of skin like clouds, but saw only thick toenails, calluses and a surprising amount of hair.

"Can I help you?"

You had come there straight from the garage roof, where you had smoked a joint and determined to make no plan whatsoever for what would happen—but still your mind had raced ahead and told stories about how it would be: he would yell at you, probably, and you'd run off; he'd ask if you were OK, and you'd say you were, and run off.

"I'm Emma," you said. "Emma James."

He looked blank. "Sorry, who?"

"Can I come in?"

You waited for him to tell you to leave. You waited for him

to threaten you, to say he would contact your parents, or the school. Instead, still looking dazed, he stepped aside.

You sat on a sagging couch while he went to the kitchen to get you a drink. You looked around. You tried to picture Mrs. Grant living in the house with him. It seemed small, and oddly dark. You had imagined she would live somewhere airy, floral, feminine. You had imagined the whole house would smell like she did, of the perfume that Caroline had confidently identified as *Allure* by Chanel, because her stepmother wore the same one. Instead, the place smelled almost of nothing, and slightly of toast.

There was a photograph of Mrs. Grant on the wall, riding a horse. Books on a shelf. An upright piano with the lid down. There was a TV in a corner of the room, squatting in a nest of cables and wires. On the screen was an image of a soldier carrying a gun, swaying and shuffling, waiting for the game to resume.

You hadn't specified what you'd like to drink, but still, you were surprised when Mr. Grant came back with two cans of lager. He handed one to you, then sat down next to you so heavily that you bounced upwards.

"Is that your piano?" you asked, nodding towards it.

"Yup," said Mr. Grant.

He picked up the Xbox controls and began to move the gunman forward on the screen. He fired the weapon and dodged and jumped over obstacles. You watched. A soundtrack of gunfire and gruff-voiced clips of speech filled a silence you nonetheless felt was strained. You waited for him to say something.

"How old are you?" you asked.

"Forty," he said.

"Is Mrs. Grant forty, too?"

He paused the game and looked across at you. "You're that girl who says hello to me outside the school."

"I say hello to everyone."

"She's forty, too," he said.

"Where is she?"

He cracked open his beer and took a long drink. You could hear the liquid in his throat, the glug of his swallowing. "She's gone. On her writing fellowship."

"Where?"

"Some island. Some unpopulated island. It's somewhere off the bottom of South America."

"Why?"

"Almost in Antarctica."

"But why?"

He drank again. "She said she wanted to concentrate. She wants to be a writer."

From the conversation on the phone, you hadn't imagined he would be this way. He had seemed softer, then, and kinder. Now, surveying him as he turned his attention back to the game, you realized that he was very drunk. His eyes were red. His thumbs were slipping off the controls.

You opened your beer and took a sip. "You don't mind that she left you behind?"

He shrugged.

"What's the matter with you?" you asked.

You weren't sure how much time had passed since you arrived. You had done a thorough survey of the living room—had scanned the bookshelf for titles you recognized and found both *The Collected Poems of Sylvia Plath* and the copy of *The Tempest*

Mrs. Grant taught from in class, had noted the pale shade of blue on the walls, the fact that you no longer smelled toast, had felt bored—and you had thought a little about your parents and whether they had been like this when they were forty. You had begun to sketch out the account of the visit you'd tell to Caroline and your other friends, in which you kissed Mr. Grant on the doorstep, and he hurried you inside to take your clothes off, and either you did have sex with him, or didn't and ran off leaving him begging you to stay. They wouldn't believe it completely but they'd want to, and nobody would dare suggest you had made it up, because the most outrageous part, really, was the fact that you had come at all, and that bit was true.

You realized then that part of you had thought, before you arrived, that you might actually have sex with Mr. Grant. You had taken a condom out of the drainpipe box and slid it into your pocket, without quite acknowledging to yourself that you were doing it. Now, you understood that nothing was going to happen, that the poems in *Tessellations* would be your only insight into the feelings Mr. Grant was capable of inspiring and the kinds of lives people like Mrs. Grant lived. It was deflating. You ran a hand across your pocket and felt the wrapper crinkle inside.

Mr. Grant's character had died in the game, and he was hunched forward, staring at the screen with no expression. He had finished his beer. He hiccupped and the back of his ribcage swelled, then fell.

There was no point waiting. Nothing else interesting was going to happen. You stood up to leave.

He lounged back on the sofa and looked up at you. "Why are you here?"

"I don't know." You pulled your hands into your sleeves.

"Of course you do."

"I read Mrs. Grant's book."

"Right. So did I."

"I'm going now."

"Are you?"

You felt as though you were pushing on a door, expecting at every moment that it would slam shut in your face, and instead it was opening wider, and behind it was an unexpected room.

"What happened to your brother?" you asked.

"What brother?"

"The brother who died."

"I don't have a brother," he said.

You sat down again.

He gave you another beer, and when you had finished that, he poured you a tumbler of whisky. You hated the taste, but swallowed anyway, because you were curious about what would happen next. Mr. Grant was still drunker than you were. He was slurring his words. He touched your knee in a way that made your skin prickle. When you told him he was more handsome with stubble than without (a kind of experiment, to see what he would do), he didn't seem awkward, and instead took your hand and lifted it to his lips.

"Why are you here?" he said again. "What do you want?"

You wriggled back from him to give yourself time to think, then decided not to think after all. You were drunk and so was he, and if he even remembered it he'd know you'd probably only said it because he had plied you with alcohol.

You said, "I want to be in love like you and Mrs. Grant."

He took hold of your hand again and squeezed it. He looked as though he might be about to laugh. He stared into your face, narrowing his eyes with a half-smile, and said, "You know, don't you, that the poems aren't real? They're just poems. She made that stuff up."

"But some of it is real," you said. "It's poetry. It's supposed to be real."

"I don't have a brother."

"Do you have vitiligo?"

"I'm not sure what that is—vitiligo."

"So it's not about you," you said. "It's not real."

He continued to squint at you. When you tried to focus on him, he had two heads, and the longer you looked, the more different they seemed: one was golden and hazy and splintered; the other like a shadow, sharper but still somehow harder to keep in focus. You wondered if you seemed the same way to him.

"I think some of it was sort of me," he said. "But it's not real life. You understand that? She made stuff up. I'm not sure she's a very good poet."

You wondered then whether you were going to vomit. You hauled yourself onto your feet and looked around for a bathroom, but your eyes were so blurry that all you could see was the dark black screen of the television. It looked like a trapdoor you could fall through.

"Hey." Mr. Grant grabbed your hand. "Where are you going?"

"I have to go," you said.

"Don't."

"I want to go," you said. Your stomach began to contract. There was a bitter taste in your mouth.

"Please," he said. He yanked your arm until you crumpled back down onto the couch. You retched, but clenched your teeth and swallowed hard before anything came up. "Don't go."

He leaned over as though he were going to kiss you, but instead wrapped his arms around your shoulders and sank down. When you tried to breathe you couldn't fill your lungs, and you wanted to yell or punch him or pinch the leg that was crushing your hand, except that you realized he had gone slack on top of you, and where his face pressed against your neck, your skin was wet, from his sweat or breath or possibly even tears, you weren't sure.

His breathing was irregular and strained. "I think she's leaving me," he whispered into your collarbone. "I don't think she's coming back from the island."

You ran home, the soles of your shoes clapping against the pavement. You went so fast you almost tripped over your own feet and sent yourself hurtling into the road, but you caught your balance at the last minute.

After a long, uncomfortable silence, Mr. Grant had fallen asleep on top of you. You had taken a full, gasping breath, which had coated your throat with the smell of his sweat and the chemical tinge of some kind of cologne. It made you cough but that didn't seem to wake him. Moments later, you managed to slide out from underneath his weight and creep across the room to the front door. He had stirred as you had turned the handle and you froze, waiting for his sighs to settle back into their wheezing rhythm, almost snores.

Later, in your bedroom, you sat with your back to the wall and your knees pulled into your chest. You called Caroline.

You, keeping your voice low so that your parents downstairs wouldn't hear: I kissed him but he was a bad kisser.

You: I feel so sorry for Mrs. Grant that she has to kiss him for the rest of her life!

You: He wanted me to stay, but I wasn't into it.

Caroline: That is so funny. That is so crazy.
You: He said Mrs. Grant is a bad poet.

At the end of the summer, you stood on the doorstep of Mr.
and Mrs. Grant's house, and rang the doorbell. You had had
an unexpected growth spurt in July, and were an inch taller
than the last time you were there. You had been on holiday
to Normandy with your parents, aunts, and cousins, and were
brown-skinned, and freckled. You had been swimming a lot,
and smoking less, and had already read the set texts for the
next school year: *Middlemarch, The Merchant of Venice,* Chaucer
and Louis MacNeice, who rhymed some of his poems and not
others. You had re-read *Tessellations* too and were coming round
to Mr. Grant's way of thinking: Mrs. Grant was not, in fact, a
very good poet. You were bored by the book. Her marriage was
not as interesting as she seemed to think it was. Why did she
imagine her life merited so much scrutiny, so much attention?
It was an ordinary life. You set your sights higher than that for
yourself.

From inside the house, you could hear footsteps approaching. The blurred outline of Mr. Grant was visible through
frosted-glass panels.

He opened the door. He was wearing proper clothes this
time: jeans and a blue shirt. He stared at you and said nothing.

"Hello, Mr. Grant. It's Emma. From before." You had worked
out a whole speech on the way over. Your message had seemed
clear then, and direct. Now, looking at Mr. Grant and the view
of the house behind him, a glimpse through a doorway of the
arm of the couch where he had fallen asleep on top of you,
clarity abandoned you. "I just came to say," you began, "that
I—" but he had already turned and walked away from the door,

leaving it ajar. You hesitated, then followed him into the living room.

He sat on the sofa with the console controls in his hand. You stood, uncertain, beside him and looked around. It was barer even than the previous time you'd been there: the books had gone from the shelf, and in their place were a few tattered magazines and a small statue of Buddha. The piano was still there, but the picture of Mrs. Grant on the horse was no longer hanging by the window. Mr. Grant moved a stack of newspapers that had been next to him on the sofa. He dropped them onto the floor with a thud and you sat in the place where they had been.

He handed you a second Xbox control. "Want to play?" he asked. "You have to choose a character."

You scrolled through the avatars on the screen: tiny men and women, different shapes and colours, and you picked one.

Punchline

I don't know how it is, I seem to be always writing about
myself. I mean all the time to write about other people,
and I try to think about myself as little as possible, and I
am sure, when I find myself coming into the story again,
I am really vexed and say, "Dear, dear, you tiresome little
creature, I wish you wouldn't!" but it is all of no use. I hope
any one who may read what I write, will understand that if
these pages contain a great deal about me, I can only
suppose it must be because I have really something to do
with them, and can't be kept out.

—ESTHER'S NARRATIVE, *BLEAK HOUSE*

Soon, a plane will arrive on the island and take me back
to Stanley. From there I will retrace the steps of my
original journey: to the airbase at Mount Pleasant,
and from Mount Pleasant to Santiago. A ten-hour overnight

layover, brief enough to make Annabel's suggestion that I "get it on" in Chile seem somewhat overambitious. A final flight that will deposit me, dazed, in London. There, I will have to fit back into the world, to find a place to live and a way to make a living, to write.

And I will have to work on this book, this new, unexpected book, in which I seem to have become the protagonist rather than Ollie.

I pack up the writing station, transforming it back into the plain, blank coffee table I had almost forgotten it originally was, so entirely consumed did it seem by the purpose I assigned it. Beneath the books, the laptop, *Bleak House*—beneath all of that writing—there was a plank of birch wood all along. I barely recognize the sunroom without my usual things there. It looks suddenly fit for purpose, with its wicker chairs and clean tables: it is waiting for guests to fill it with conversation and laughter and smells; it is waiting for the sun.

It takes no time at all to pack, and when I'm done my suitcase still looks empty: gone are the bags of food that occupied most of the space on the way here. They have vanished into me. Gone, too, is the BU sweatshirt that I last saw clinging, sodden, to the tussac by Long Gulch. The CDs I have acquired do little to restore balance.

Like the case, I too am lighter. My jeans have been held up with a piece of string for the past couple of weeks. At the airport in Stanley, forty-one days ago, the woman who checked me in weighed me with my luggage, and then asked me to estimate how much lighter my bag would be on the return journey. I gave what I thought was a perfectly accurate answer, since I knew the exact weight of the food I was carrying, and that it would be gone by the time I left. But I hadn't considered, in that calculation, that I would be lighter too. Bits of me — the layers of fat on my stomach, hips and thighs — have disappeared on the island.

Other things that no longer exist: my wild determination to write the Ollie novel; my belief that it can be a success.

These losses, and the accompanying sensation of lightness, strike me, now, as positive changes. I have freed myself of a bad book. I will write a better book now. I don't know when, or how, but I know I will write it.

I set my notebooks down on top of the remaining clothes and think how strange it is that they don't take up more room, or at the very least, that they don't weigh more now that they're full of words.

I walk up the hill to George and Alison's house to say goodbye. I thank them for their hospitality, their generosity, their good humour. I thank them for teaching me the names of birds, and how to herd pregnant cows through a gate. I promise to send them a copy of my book when it's finished, and don't mention that it won't be quite what I told them it would be.

Just before I leave, I give Alison back the potato. It is wrinkled. It has begun to sprout green tentacles. I am embarrassed — I considered at first walking over to the cliffs, or to Long Gulch, and hurling it into the water, but it seemed such a shame to waste it, when vegetables are so precious here, when I know Alison will be able to turn it into something edible. Fortunately, she is amused, rather than offended.

"You don't like potatoes?" she asks.

"I just didn't need it," I say.

The plane that takes me away from Bleaker is full — which means there are three other people on board — and I sit up front, next to the pilot, as I did on my way here. The controls are right in front of me, and I have to wear an enormous head-set with a microphone. I wonder what useful comments I can be expected to offer as we fly.

The pilot asks me to refrain from pushing either of two pedals, pulling this lever, or pressing that button. I feel certain that something is going to possess me to do all of these things as soon as we take off, and sit on my hands.

From above, Bleaker looks disconcertingly tame. Long Gulch is a cranny; Big Pond a puddle; the North End a neat grey cap that sits atop the green tip of the island. The red-roofed buildings of the settlement look like Monopoly hotels: flimsy. I peer out of the window and think that inside one of them George and Alison are likely standing at the window, waving. The beach curves like an open parenthesis, its ends reaching towards the Antarctic. I crane my neck around as we fly, but soon all I can see is grey rock and grey water and I know that, if I am honest, I can't tell which is which.

The flight takes a long route all around the islands and West Falkland before heading back to town. There are deliveries to make: food, post, news. Below us the landscape is murky and strange and soon, as we reach West Falkland, immense. There is so much more here than my tiny island, than the view from the sunroom of the bay and the whale skeleton and the circling caracaras. We fly low over jagged rock formations and land on muddy airstrips; people amble out from houses enclosed for miles by nothing but hills and water. They collect their mail and freight, then vanish back into private wildernesses. While I was fretting and analysing my isolation on Bleaker, I was surrounded by other people who seem to take these conditions entirely in their stride. For each island, an inhabitant, or maybe two or three. For me, it was an experiment. For them, it is the fact and material of their lives.

At the very end of "Tips for Writing and Life," Leslie throws in a new rule: "Do not look into your own heart and write; look into someone else's." This comes back to me, now, as we thud down beside another settlement, and a new cast of strange faces appears and make its way towards the plane.

No matter where we land, however desolate and remote it appears, the people we meet know exactly who I am. Word of the American authoress on Bleaker has spread throughout the Falklands. These red-faced, rough-handed, mysterious strangers ask, each time, about the progress of my history book.

"It's coming along nicely," I say. "Yes, it was, it was very relaxing on Bleaker. I got a lot done."

I had such good intentions of following Leslie's last rule. I was so certain I was looking into someone else's heart.

Now if truth be told, I violate a good many of these rules (for example, I'm always saying, "Do not look into your own heart and write; look into someone else's"—this from a man who recently wrote an autobiographical novel). So may you. But you ought at least to be aware that you are doing so and be able to justify each such decision. It's possible to take everything I've said both with a grain of salt and not lightly. That's the kind of balancing act all good writing consists of. (Note how I've just begun one sentence with a conjunction and used a preposition to end another, and thrown in parentheses to boot—none of them good ideas.) I wish you luck upon the high wire.

—"Tips for Writing and Life," Leslie Epstein

. . .

We are heading back to Stanley now. I can see, ahead of us, the lighthouse on the tip of East Falkland, and beyond it, a disturbance of the beige sweep of land: the crinkled rooftops of the town. My mind is darting all over the place — to what I'm going to eat first, to who I'm going to call first, to the clothes I can now wear that aren't rigorously practical — and I don't immediately notice that the pilot is trying to attract my attention.

"Nell! Nell!"

His voice is buzzing in my headphones. After multiple descents and ascents in the plane, my ears have popped and I am almost deaf.

"Nell," he says again, once I've turned to look at him. "Tell me something."

He has one hand on the controls. The other is unwrapping a ham sandwich from tinfoil.

"Sure," I say.

"What's the punchline?"

"The punchline?"

"You know," he says, taking a bite of his sandwich. "The punchline of the book."

I adjust my microphone to buy myself time as I consider the idea that the entirety of my book should hinge on a single line, and then I say, "I wish I knew."

The pilot roars with laughter and slaps his thigh; the plane wobbles in the air. He wipes his eyes. He's still chuckling to himself and shaking his head as we begin our final descent. "All that time by herself on an island," he says, "and she don't even know the punchline."

Afterwards

dream and dream of Bleaker Island. I dream I am still there, that I never left and am sitting on the beach waiting for a plane that doesn't come. Or I dream that I'm being sent back, because I didn't finish the novel; I am scared of the weather and the hunger and I don't have time to pack the right things before I leave. I dream that I take my friends there to show them around, only to find that everything has changed: a city has grown up beside the cliffs; there are roads now, and trains, and tower blocks, and my friends say, "Oh, this isn't how you described it at all."

It is four hundred and ninety-eight days since I left Bleaker. I am sitting in the kitchen of a small flat in South London, which is where I live now—alone, surrounded by the city. I have a fridge stacked with food, a fruit bowl full of mottled bananas. There are wine glasses by the sink with discs of Malbec crusting in the bottom, left over from a dinner party two nights ago. All around me are the noises of people nearby living lives: music seeping from car windows, doors slamming, babies crying and a single, clear cough on the other side of a wall. I have continuous access to the Internet now; I can google anything that pops into my mind. I have a functioning phone. If I want to speak to someone, all I have to do is tap the screen.

The island is half a world away and feels further. It is hard to hold it all in my mind at once—that I was there, am now here—and I worry sometimes that it is slipping from my reach. What if, after the initial shock of the hubbub of the rest of the world, after a few days of gluttony when I ate my weight in carbohydrates, after learning to restrain the urge to talk to myself in public places—what if after that, not much is left from those weeks I spent at the bottom of the world? What if the reason my dreams keep dragging me back there is that I didn't get enough out of it, didn't do enough, didn't take enough away? What was the point of it all?

I open a new notebook on the first page and gaze at it. It looks like all the other blank pages I've confronted in my life and eventually filled. On this one I write, "Things I Learned on Bleaker Island."

· You have to try really hard;
· But sometimes trying really hard is the least effective thing to do.
· Hunger is not good discipline.
· Discipline is writing a new book when the previous one fails.
· Discipline is the opposite of loneliness.

I like to think I am not the kind of person who has epiphanies on an island. I did not go to Bleaker to bring back an illuminating dispatch from the South Atlantic. I just wanted to write a book. I'd been trying, in various ways, to write books my whole life, and this was another attempt. And in the end, isn't it true that I did what I set out to do? I did write a book. Not the book I had planned, but a book, all the same, which came together quickly and decidedly, in the space of a few days about a year after I got home. I curled up on my sofa with my knees to my chest and my laptop on my feet, the frantic soundtrack from the film *Whiplash* playing in the background, and I took all the things I did and thought and dreamed and remembered and imagined on Bleaker Island, all those diary entries and panicked scraps of writing, and I put them together, side by side. I joined them up and smoothed them out and cut down the number of times I complained about the Internet, and then I gave it the title of the novel that never quite came to be.

The punchline is that I did leave the island with a book.

· Solitude is the contented twin of loneliness.
· Variety is a kind of company.
· Everything is a kind of work.
· Do not look into your own heart and write, but do not be surprised if you end up there all the same.
· Despite what you might think—despite what Ted Hughes might lead you to believe—there is no such thing as effortless concentration.

The list of things I learned grows: bullet points listing the point of it all. And it isn't over yet. It keeps happening. When I wake up alone in my flat on a Saturday morning, and slide into yet another blank page, which I spend the whole day filling, and then, after hours by myself, I go out to meet friends, to eat and drink and talk, it feels so obvious now that it is possible, necessary even, to be alone and not alone all in the space of a day. When I send the manuscript of my memoir out to agents, I find someone who understands not just what the book is, but also what I am under the impression that it is, and knows how to bridge the gap between the two. When I concentrate, it is not effortlessly, but with great effort. When, at a party, someone asks me what I do, I say, "I'm a writer," without hesitation or blushing or feeling that I am lying. I am a writer. So *this* is the point, I think, in meetings with editors; jotting down ideas for stories on the Tube; when I wake from a dream about riots in the centre of the bed. All of it is, but specifically: this.

Acknowledgements

Leslie Epstein showed me what a writer is, in writing and in life. Sigrid Nunez and Ha Jin taught me more about telling stories in one year than I had gleaned from the previous twenty-six put together. The support of Maureen Freely has been invaluable. Louise Tondeur helped me at just the right time.

Robert Hildreth established the Global Fellowship programme at Boston University and in doing so made my journey to the Falklands—and the existence of this book—possible. I am grateful, too, for the Marcia Trimble Fellowship and the Florence Engel Randall Award, which supported me during my MFA.

I am indebted to the people in the Falklands, and on Bleaker Island in particular, who hosted me during my stay. I was, and continue to be, inspired by their warmth, strength and good humour.

My classmates at BU shared honest criticism and abundant

ideas over the course of many hours in Room 222. In particular, Cara Bayles and Chris Amenta deserve thanks for their clear vision, brutal edits and big hearts.

Without Laura Marris, nothing I write would ever have a title, and everything would be worse.

Amanda Walker, Claudia Gray and Grace Shortland have thrilled, humoured, challenged, supported, laughed at and laughed with me since our very first class together in the art block: full enjoy.

Gabrielle Mearns remembers the events described in this book far better than I do, and offered humour, perspective and love through them all.

Camilla Hornby took a chance on a wandering twenty-three-year-old.

Hannah Griffiths was generous and wise.

A phenomenal trio of editors brought this book to life. Sophie Jonathan, Kris Puopolo and Lynn Henry were inventive, insightful, patient, and visionary as they cajoled my manuscript into shape.

Rebecca Carter, my agent at Janklow & Nesbit, knows what I want to say long before I've found a way to say it. She transformed a series of anecdotes into the book I had imagined but didn't know how to write. Emma Parry at Janklow & Nesbit's American office told me I was a real writer now, and was instrumental in making that the case.

If I had not made a project of copying Simon Stevens from a young age, I would have much less to say.

My parents, Margaret and Richard, read not only bedtime stories but daytime ones, and made everything possible. Thank you.

Without Brendan Hare this book would not exist.